THE WELLNESS PARADIGM

Mastering The Art Of Mental, Emotional, Physical And Spiritual Awakening

---

Tarrent- 'Authur 'Henry

Copyright © 2023 Tarrent-'Authur' Henry

ISBN 978-2-3377-1977-0 (paperback)

ISBN 978-2-0599-1686-0 (e-book)

TABLE OF CONTENTS

INTRODUCTION

Congratulations on purchasing "The Wellness Paradigm: Mastering the Art of Mental, Emotional, Physical and Spiritual Awakening." As you hold this book in your hands, you are one step closer to becoming the person you've always wanted to be—a mentally, emotionally, physically, and spiritually well individual with a profound relationship with God. Now, let's embark on a journey together to unlock the tools and wisdom needed to bring about the transformation you desire.

Unwrapping the Contents

In these pages, you will find practical advice, tips, and relatable examples that will guide you towards a state of total well-being. By drawing on my credentials as a best-selling author, mental wellness expert, coach, speaker, trainer, and Spiritual Leader. I aim to provide you with a comprehensive roadmap to becoming the ideal human you have always desired to be.

Key Themes Explored

Mastering Mental Wellness: Understanding the intricate workings of the mind is crucial to nurturing mental well-being. Through insightful guidance and exercises, we will delve into stress management, meditation, and mindfulness.

Cultivating Emotional Intelligence: Developing emotional intelligence enables us to navigate complex feelings, build healthier relationships, and harness positivity. It allows us to embrace vulnerability, authenticity, and empathy so we can thrive emotionally.

Nurturing Physical Well-being: Our bodies are sacred vessels, and caring for them is vital to overall wellness. This section will equip you with actionable steps for proper nutrition, regular exercise, restful sleep, and maintaining an optimal work-life balance.

Connecting with Your Spiritual Side: Strengthening your relationship with God is an essential component of the wellness paradigm. Discover ways to deepen your spirituality, whether through prayer, meditation, or engaging in practices that align with your personal beliefs. You will find peace, purpose, and guidance as you embark on this transformative spiritual journey.

Embracing Your Ideal Self

Throughout this book, my goal is to empower you with the necessary tools to shape your life in alignment with your unique purpose. By the time you're done reading, you'll be equipped with practical strategies to navigate life's challenges, embrace your vulnerabilities, and thrive in all aspects of your being.

Friendly Encouragement

So, take a deep breath, anchor yourself in hope, and let's embark on this transformative journey of becoming the ideal human you always wanted to be.

As you read "The Wellness Paradigm: Mastering the Art of Mental, Emotional, Physical and Spiritual Awakening," allow yourself to absorb the wisdom contained within these pages. Remember, you already have the book in your hands; now it's time to immerse yourself in its transformative power.

Let's harness the spectrum of mental, emotional, physical, and spiritual wellness, igniting the flame of personal growth and fostering an unbreakable bond with the divine.

It's time to claim your destiny and live as the ideal human you were always meant to be. So go ahead, begin your journey, and unlock the incredible potential that lies within you.

CHAPTER ONE

The Incredible Journey to Wholeness: *A Personal Account of Achieving Wellness and Deepening Your Faith*

"Wellness is the result of mindful choices we make towards a healthy lifestyle." - Anonymous

My journey has been a comprehensive and multi-faceted one, and it exemplifies the principles and practices I recommend to those seeking to become the ideal, well-rounded human being they aspire to be. I firmly believe that mental wellness is the foundation upon which all other aspects of our well-being are built. For me, this journey started with a commitment to constantly educate myself and develop my cognitive abilities.

I immersed myself in books on psychology, neuroscience, and cognitive science, seeking to understand the mind's inner workings. This quest for knowledge led me to practice mindfulness meditation, which has proven to be an invaluable tool in managing and regulating my thoughts and emotions. Emotional wellness, for me, came hand in hand with mental wellness. By understanding the interplay between our thoughts, emotions, and behaviors, I was able to cultivate emotional intelligence and resilience.

This involved deep introspection, and applying various techniques such as journaling, self-reflection, and emotional regulation exercises. I also recognized the importance of creating and maintaining healthy relationships, surrounding myself with positive influences, and engaging in meaningful connections with others. Physical wellness has been another crucial component of my journey towards holistic well-being. I adopted a disciplined exercise approach, incorporating cardiovascular activities, strength training, and flexibility exercises into my routine.

Moreover, I prioritized proper nutrition, ensuring a well-balanced diet that fuels both my body and mind. This synthesis of physical activity and healthy eating has led to increased energy, improved mood, and enhanced cognitive functioning. Lastly, spiritual wellness and developing a strong relationship with God have been indispensable in achieving the level of fulfillment and purpose I sought.

I devoted time to studying various religious and spiritual traditions, seeking not only knowledge but also a personal connection with a higher power. Through prayer, meditation, and deep reflection, I cultivated a sense of transcendence, recognizing the profound nature of existence beyond the material realm. This spiritual connection has provided me with guidance, comfort, and a sense of inner peace during challenging times.

In summary, my journey towards mental, emotional, physical, and spiritual wellness, as well as establishing a strong relationship with God, has been a deliberate and intentional pursuit. It required a commitment to lifelong learning, consistent self-reflection, and the application of evidence-based practices. By developing each aspect of my being, I have experienced greater fulfillment, happiness, and a deeper connection with God. I encourage you to embrace a multifaceted approach, recognizing the interconnectedness of these dimensions and the potential for transformative growth.

Wellness Practices

1. **Mental Wellness:** One example of practicing mental wellness is engaging in cognitive exercises and puzzles to sharpen and expand the mind. This could include regularly solving Sudoku or crossword puzzles, learning a new language, or participating in brain-training apps or games. **Emotional Wellness:** Practice gratitude and positive thinking. Keep a gratitude journal and regularly write down three things you are grateful for each day. Challenge negative thoughts by replacing them with positive affirmations.

2. **Physical Wellness:** Incorporate regular exercise into your routine. You could go jogging or walking outside. Consider going to the gym or attending fitness classes.

3. **Spiritual Wellness:** Find a quiet place and spend time in prayer and meditation. Sit in silence, focus on your breathing, and 'turn off your brain, and listen to God'.

4. **Establishing a Relationship with God:** A strong relationship with God involves attending religious services or gatherings regularly. Participating in community service or volunteer work. Bible study and sound biblical teaching to deepen your understanding and connection with God. These examples highlight the various ways in which you can actively pursue mental, emotional, physical, and spiritual wellness and develop a strong relationship with God.

Now that we have explored some examples of how individuals can cultivate mental, emotional, physical, and spiritual wellness, and establish a relationship with God, let's dive into a case study that demonstrates the transformative power of these practices.

Sarah is a 35-year-old woman who has embarked on a journey toward achieving mental, emotional, physical, and spiritual wellness and establishing a strong relationship with God. She believes that these dimensions are interconnected and vital for a well-rounded and fulfilled life. Sarah's case study exemplifies the principles and practices she has implemented in her pursuit of holistic well-being.

Actions and Initiatives Implemented

1. **Mental Wellness:** Sarah committed to constant education and self-improvement by immersing herself in books on psychology, neuroscience, and cognitive science. She also practiced mindfulness meditation to manage and regulate her thoughts and emotions effectively.
2. **Emotional Wellness:** Sarah recognized the interplay between thoughts, emotions, and behaviors, leading her to cultivate emotional intelligence and resilience. She engaged in therapy, practiced deep introspection, and utilized techniques like journaling, self-reflection, and emotional regulation exercises. Sarah also prioritized healthy relationships and meaningful connections.
3. **Physical Wellness:** Sarah adopted a disciplined approach to exercise, incorporating cardiovascular activities, strength training, and flexibility exercises into her routine. She also focused on maintaining a well-balanced diet to fuel her body and mind effectively.
4. **Spiritual Wellness:** Sarah devoted time to studying and learning about God, seeking knowledge and a personal connection. She practiced prayer, meditation, and deep reflection to cultivate a life built on faith and inner peace.

Measurable Outcomes Achieved

1. **Mental Wellness:** Sarah experienced improved cognitive abilities and greater control over her thoughts and emotions because of her commitment to education and mindfulness meditation.

2. **Emotional Wellness:** Sarah developed emotional intelligence and resilience, enabling her to navigate and manage her emotions effectively. She established and maintained healthy relationships and experienced meaningful connections with others.
3. **Physical Wellness:** Sarah's disciplined approach to exercise and proper nutrition led to increased energy, improved mood, and enhanced cognitive functioning.
4. **Spiritual Wellness:** Sarah's spiritual practices, including prayer, meditation, and Bible study, provided her with guidance, comfort, and a sense of inner peace during challenging times.

Challenges Faced

Sarah faced various challenges throughout her wellness journey. She encountered resistance from within herself, as old habits and patterns proved challenging to overcome. Societal pressures and external influences sometimes hindered her progress. It was also challenging for Sarah to find a balance between her commitments and dedicating time to self-care and spiritual practices.

Lessons Learned

Holistic well-being requires a multifaceted approach, addressing mental, emotional, physical, and spiritual dimensions simultaneously. Lifelong learning and consistent self-reflection are crucial for personal growth and development. One's environment and relationships play a vital role in overall wellness, necessitating the cultivation of healthy connections and positive influences. Balancing commitments and self-care are essential to ensure sustained progress and avoid burnout.

Overall Assessment of Impact

Sarah's commitment to pursuing mental, emotional, physical, and spiritual wellness, as well as establishing a strong relationship with God, has had a profound impact on her life. She experienced greater fulfillment, happiness, improved relationships, enhanced cognitive functioning, and a deeper connection with God. Sarah's well-rounded approach to wellness has transformed her overall well-being, allowing her to live a more purposeful and meaningful life. She encourages others to embrace a similar multifaceted approach and recognizes the transformative potential of such a journey.

Typical Mistakes and How to Avoid Them

1. **Neglecting mental wellness:** Many people fail to recognize the importance of mental wellness as the foundation for overall well-being. To avoid this mistake, you should prioritize educating yourself, developing cognitive abilities, and practicing mindfulness meditation to manage thoughts and emotions.

2. **Overlooking emotional wellness:** Emotional wellness is often intertwined with mental wellness. You should strive to understand the interplay between thoughts, emotions, and behaviors, and cultivate emotional intelligence and resilience through introspection, therapy, journaling, self-reflection, and emotional regulation exercises.

3. **Ignoring physical wellness:** Physical wellness is a crucial aspect of holistic well-being. You should adopt a disciplined approach to exercise, which includes cardiovascular activities, strength training, and flexibility exercises. Prioritizing a well-balanced diet and proper nutrition is also essential for increased energy, improved mood, and enhanced cognitive functioning.

4. **Neglecting spiritual wellness:** Developing a strong relationship with God and achieving spiritual wellness is often overlooked. Engaging in prayer, meditation, and deep reflection is important to cultivate a sense of transcendence and find inner peace during challenging times.

My #1 Piece of Advice

My biggest piece of advice to you who are seeking to become mentally, emotionally, physically, and spiritually well is to prioritize self-care and practice self-compassion. This involves taking intentional time for rest, engaging in activities that bring you joy, nurturing healthy relationships, seeking professional help if needed, and nurturing your spiritual connection with God through prayer and meditation.

***Remember, you are worthy of love and care, and by prioritizing your well-being, you can start your journey toward a healthier and more fulfilling life.**

Summary

- Embrace a comprehensive approach to well-being, focusing on mental, emotional, physical, and spiritual wellness.

- Commit to lifelong learning, expanding knowledge of psychology, neuroscience, and cognitive science.

- Practice mindfulness meditation to manage and regulate thoughts and emotions.

- Cultivate emotional intelligence and resilience through introspection, therapy, journaling, and emotional regulation exercises.

- Prioritize physical wellness through disciplined exercise routines and a well-balanced diet for increased energy and improved cognitive functioning.

Quiz

1. What is the foundation upon which all other aspects of well-being are built?

    A. Emotional wellness

    B. Physical wellness

    C. Mental wellness

    D. Spiritual wellness

2. What are some techniques used to cultivate emotional intelligence and resilience?
    A. Exercise and nutrition
    B. Mindfulness meditation
    C. Deep introspection and journaling
    D. Establishing healthy relationships

3. What is a recommended approach to physical wellness?
    A. Regular exercise and proper nutrition
    B. A well-balanced diet
    C. Engaging in meaningful connections
    D. Creating positive influences

4. What is an important factor in achieving spiritual wellness?
    A. Establishing a personal connection with a higher power
    B. Understanding the interplay between thoughts, emotions, and behaviors
    C. Practicing mindfulness meditation
    D. Developing cognitive abilities

5. What is the benefit of a multifaceted approach to achieving holistic well-being?
    A. Increased energy and improved mood
    B. A deeper connection with the divine
    C. Recognizing the interconnectedness of different dimensions

D. Greater fulfillment and purpose

Answer Key

1. C

2. C & D

3. A & B

4. A

5. C & D

Now that I have shared my journey toward wellness and my relationship with God, I want to show you practical examples of daily habits and routines that have helped me maintain my mental, emotional, physical, and spiritual well-being, so keep reading to discover the keys to a balanced and fulfilling life.

CHAPTER TWO

The Four Pillars of Well-Being: Daily Habits for a Strong Relationship with God

"Your habits determine your character, and your character determines your destiny." - Zig Ziglar

Developing daily habits or routines that promote mental, emotional, physical, and spiritual well-being is essential for individuals seeking a strong relationship with God. By incorporating these habits into one's daily life, you can improve your overall well-being, enhance your connection with God, and experience a deeper sense of purpose and fulfillment.

1. **Meditation and Prayer:** Engaging in regular meditation and prayer can have a profound impact on one's mental, emotional, and spiritual wellness. Taking the time to quiet the mind and connect with God allows you to find a sense of peace and clarity amidst the chaos of daily life.

2. **Daily Scripture Reading:** Devoting time each day to reading and reflecting upon scriptures can significantly contribute to your spiritual growth and understanding. Scripture reading provides guidance, inspiration, and a deeper understanding of God's teachings. Engaging with the Word of God daily can bring about a sense of purpose, comfort, and wisdom.

3. **Physical Exercise and Self-Care:** Maintaining a healthy lifestyle by incorporating physical exercise and proper self-care is essential for overall well-being. Regular exercise not only benefits the body but also has a positive impact on your mental and emotional health. Physical activity releases endorphins, reduces stress, boosts mood, and improves cognitive function. Additionally, practicing self-care activities, such as getting enough sleep, eating nutritious meals, and engaging in hobbies, can help you recharge and nurture your overall well-being.

4. **Community Engagement:** Active participation in a community of like-minded individuals who share similar values and spiritual beliefs is vital for fostering a strong relationship with God. Engaging in regular fellowship, attending religious services, and joining small groups or prayer

circles can provide a sense of belonging and support. Being part of a community encourages spiritual growth, accountability, and the opportunity to serve others.

5. **Journaling and Reflection:** Carving out time each day for personal reflection and journaling serves as a powerful tool for self-discovery, and emotional and spiritual growth. Writing down thoughts, prayers, and reflections on daily experiences can help you process emotions, gain clarity, and deepen your connection with God. Journaling enables you to identify patterns, celebrate growth, and seek guidance, ultimately leading to a more profound relationship with God and increased emotional well-being. It is important to note that while these habits can be tremendously beneficial, it is essential to approach them with genuine intention and follow established procedures or guidelines for authenticity and accuracy. By embracing these practices and integrating them into daily routines, you can develop a strong relationship with God and foster your mental, emotional, physical, and spiritual well-being.

Now that we have explored the importance of developing daily habits for a strong relationship with God, let's look at the checklist I have created to help you incorporate these habits into your daily life.

1. Set aside a specific time each day for meditation and prayer.

2. Create a quiet and comfortable space for meditation and prayer.

3. A daily scripture reading plan or choose passages to reflect on each day.

4. Find a physical exercise routine that you enjoy and commit to doing it regularly.

5. Prioritize self-care activities such as getting enough sleep, eating nutritious meals, and engaging in hobbies.

6. Seek out a community of like-minded individuals with similar values and beliefs.

7. Attend religious services and participate in fellowship opportunities.

8. Consider joining a small group or prayer circle for deeper connection and support.

9. Carve out time each day for personal reflection and journaling.

10. Write down thoughts, prayers, and reflections on daily experiences to process emotions and connect with God.

These action steps can be tailored and personalized to suit your preferences and needs. It is important to approach these habits with sincerity and adapt them to your unique circumstances and beliefs.

Now that we have discussed the checklist for developing daily habits for mental, emotional, physical, and spiritual well-being, let's look at some examples that demonstrate how these action steps can be implemented in practical life.

1. **Gratitude Practice:** Cultivating a daily practice of gratitude helps you focus on the positive aspects of your life and acknowledge the blessings you have received from God. Expressing gratitude through prayers, journaling, or sharing with others fosters a sense of contentment, joy, and humility.

2. **Acts of Service:** Engaging in acts of service and kindness towards others not only helps them but also deepens your relationship with God. Volunteering at a local charity, helping a friend in need, or simply practicing random acts of kindness can bring about a sense of purpose, compassion, and fulfillment.

3. **Mindful Eating:** Paying attention to the food we eat and practicing mindful eating can serve as a spiritual practice. By focusing on each bite, expressing gratitude for the nourishment, and being aware of the body's hunger and fullness cues, you can develop a deeper appreciation for the connection between your physical and spiritual well-being.

4. **Nature Connection:** Spending time in nature and appreciating God's creation can be a powerful source of spiritual nourishment. Going for walks, hikes, or simply sitting outdoors and observing the beauty of the natural world can help you feel connected to God, find solace, and gain perspective.

5. **Silence and Solitude:** Taking regular breaks from noise, distractions, and technology to be alone with your thoughts and feelings can foster a deeper sense of spiritual connection. Embracing silence and solitude allows you to listen to that **Inner Voice**, reflect on your values, and cultivate a deeper understanding of yourself and your relationship with God.

Now that we have explored some examples of spiritual practices that can deepen one's connection with God, let's dive into a case study that illustrates the transformative power of these practices in one individual's life.

Mark is a 40-year-old individual who has always felt a deep desire to develop a strong relationship with God. However, due to the demands of his busy lifestyle, Mark has struggled to find the time and consistency needed to nurture his spiritual well-being. Feeling unfulfilled and disconnected, Mark commits to incorporating daily habits that can help him deepen his connection with God and cultivate overall well-being.

Actions and Initiatives Implemented

1. **Meditation and Prayer:** Mark starts each day by dedicating 15 minutes to meditation and prayer. He finds a quiet space in his home, focuses on his breath, and surrenders his thoughts and worries to God. Mark uses prayer to express gratitude, seek guidance, and connect with a higher power. **Daily Scripture Reading:** Mark sets aside time in the morning and evening to read and reflect upon scripture. He selects key verses or passages from the Bible and spends 20 minutes contemplating their meaning and applying them to his life. This daily practice allows Mark to gain wisdom, find comfort, and align his actions with his faith.

2. **Physical Exercise and Self-Care:** Recognizing the importance of physical well-being, Mark incorporates regular exercise into his routine. He joins a local gym and commits to exercising for 30 minutes, five days a week. Mark also prioritizes self-care by ensuring he gets enough sleep, eats nutritious meals, and engages in activities that bring him joy.

3. **Community Engagement:** Mark seeks out a community of individuals who share his spiritual beliefs. He joins a church and participates in weekly services. Additionally, Mark becomes involved in a small group dedicated to studying and discussing scripture. Through community engagement, Mark finds support, accountability, and opportunities to serve others, which deepens his connection with God

4. **Journaling and Reflection:** To further enhance his spiritual growth, Mark starts journaling daily. He writes down his thoughts, prayers, and reflections on his experiences. This practice allows Mark to process emotions, gain clarity, and seek guidance from God. Journaling serves as a valuable tool for self-discovery and emotional well-being.

Measurable Outcomes Achieved

1. **Reduced stress and increased emotional well-being:** Regular meditation, prayer, and journaling help Mark manage his emotions, leading to decreased stress and increased emotional regulation.
2. **Deeper sense of purpose and fulfillment:** Engaging with scripture and reflecting on its teachings gives Mark a sense of direction, purpose, and fulfillment in his daily life.
3. **Improved physical health:** Incorporating exercise and self-care practices into his routine improves Mark's physical health, boosting his energy levels and overall well-being.
4. **Increased sense of belonging and support:** Being part of a spiritual community allows Mark to feel a sense of belonging and find support in his spiritual journey.

Challenges Faced

1. **Time management:** Initially, Mark struggles to find time for these daily habits due to his busy schedule. However, by prioritizing and creating a schedule, Mark gradually manages to incorporate these practices into his routine.
2. **Maintaining consistency:** Mark sometimes faces days when he feels unmotivated or overwhelmed. During these times, he reminds himself of the importance of these habits and pushes through, knowing that consistency is key to developing a strong relationship with God.

Lessons Learned

1. **Consistency is key:** Establishing daily habits requires commitment and consistency. Building a strong relationship with God involves making these practices a priority and dedicating time to them every day

2. **Flexibility and adaptability:** Mark realizes that these habits may need to be adjusted as his life circumstances change. Being open to adapting the routines ensures that they continue to serve his spiritual growth.

3. **Connecting with like-minded individuals:** Joining a spiritual community provides invaluable support, encouragement, and accountability, enhancing the development of a strong relationship with God.

Overall Assessment of Impact

Through the implementation of daily habits, Mark experiences a profound impact on his life. His relationship with God deepens, resulting in a greater sense of peace, purpose, and fulfillment. Mark's mental, emotional, physical, and spiritual well-being improved significantly, enabling him to navigate life's challenges with resilience and a deeper connection to his faith. By fostering these habits, Mark transforms his daily life, cultivating a strong and meaningful relationship with God.

Typical Mistakes and How to Avoid Them

Lack of consistency: You may start with good intentions but fail to consistently practice these habits. To avoid this, it is important to prioritize these habits and set aside dedicated time each day for their practice. **Neglecting self-care:** You may often overlook the importance of physical exercise and self-care in your daily routines. To avoid this mistake, you should make self-care activities and physical exercise a priority, just like other spiritual practices.

Not seeking guidance or support: You may try to navigate your spiritual journey alone or without seeking guidance from experienced mentors or joining a community. To avoid this, it is crucial to actively engage in a community of like-minded individuals and seek guidance from spiritual leaders or mentors. **Poor Bible study habits:** You may read scriptures without deeply reflecting upon them or understanding their teachings. To avoid this, you should approach scripture reading with a mindset of reflection and seek to understand the deeper meanings and lessons.

Lack of self-reflection and introspection: It is common for you to neglect regular self-reflection and journaling, which are essential for personal growth and spiritual development. To avoid this mistake, you should prioritize time for personal reflection and make journaling a daily practice.

My #1 Piece of Advice

Be consistent in prayer, meditation, reading scriptures, and practicing gratitude to strengthen your relationship with God.

Summary

- Cultivate inner peace and clarity through regular meditation and prayer sessions, allowing for a deeper connection with God amidst life's chaos.

- Experience spiritual growth and understanding by making daily scripture reading and reflection a priority, finding guidance, inspiration, and wisdom in the Word of God.

- Enhance overall well-being by incorporating physical exercise and self-care practices into your daily routine, benefiting not only your body but also your mental and emotional health.

- Foster a strong relationship with God by actively engaging in a like-minded community, attending religious services, and participating in small groups that provide support and encouragement on your spiritual journey.

- Deepen your connection with God through the power of journaling and reflection, using this transformative tool for self-discovery, emotional regulation, and spiritual growth.

Quiz

1. Is it important to develop daily habits or routines that promote mental, emotional, physical, and spiritual well-being to have a strong relationship with God?
2. What can regular meditation and prayer sessions do to one's mental, emotional, and spiritual well-being?
3. How can Scripture reading contribute to one's spiritual growth and understanding?
4. What are the benefits of physical exercise on mental and emotional health?
5. How can active participation in a community of like-minded individuals foster a strong relationship with God?

Answer Key

1. Absolutely
2. Reduce stress, and anxiety, and even improve cognitive function and emotional regulation
3. Guidance, inspiration, and a deeper understanding of God's teachings
4. Releases endorphins, reduces stress, boosts mood, and improves cognitive function
5. Fostering a strong relationship with God

Now that we have explored the numerous daily habits and routines that foster overall well-being, it is vital to delve deeper into the transformative power of mindfulness and meditation, which can greatly enhance our mental, emotional, and spiritual health.

So, grab a cozy spot, and let's continue our journey towards a more enriched and balanced life together.

CHAPTER THREE

Unveiling the Ideal Human: Characteristics of a Strong Relationship with God

"Faith is taking the first step even when you don't see the whole staircase." -Martin Luther King Jr.

When defining the ideal human with a strong relationship with God, it is important to consider the characteristics and qualities that would make you stand out. A strong relationship with God encompasses not only religious beliefs but also a deep spiritual connection and a commitment to living a life guided by religious values.

1. **Faith and Trust:** An ideal human with a strong relationship with God should have unwavering faith and trust in the divine. This entails believing in the existence of God and having confidence in His power and guidance. It also involves surrendering to God's will and accepting that He has a plan for you.

2. **Devotion and Worship:** An ideal human with a strong relationship with God should demonstrate devotion and consistent acts of worship. This includes regular prayer, attending religious services, and engaging in personal spiritual practices. Worshiping God with sincerity and reverence shows a deep commitment to the relationship and demonstrates the desire to connect with the divine.

3. **Moral and Ethical Living:** Living a life by moral and ethical principles is a crucial aspect of maintaining a strong relationship with God. An ideal human with a strong relationship with God should possess qualities such as honesty, integrity, compassion, forgiveness, and love towards others. Upholding these values reflects your commitment to leading a righteous and virtuous life.

4. **Humility:** Humility is an essential characteristic for humans with a strong relationship with God. Recognizing that you are merely a creation of a higher power leads to a sense of humility, acknowledging that you are not above others and that your accomplishments are a gift from God. Humility also involves being willing to learn, grow, and lean on the guidance provided by God.

5. **Gratitude:** An ideal human with a strong relationship with God should possess an attitude of gratitude. Gratitude towards God for blessings, both big and small, fosters a sense of appreciation and recognition of the divine in your life. Expressing gratitude through prayers, actions, and a positive mindset further strengthens the bond with God.

6. **Service to Others:** Serving others and making a positive impact on the world is another vital quality of an ideal human with a strong relationship with God. By engaging in acts of kindness, giving to those in need, and showing compassion towards others, you demonstrate your love for God through selfless actions.

7. **Seeking Knowledge and Understanding:** Pursuing knowledge and understanding of your faith is crucial for developing a strong relationship with God. Reading religious texts and seeking guidance from knowledgeable individuals help to deepen your understanding of God's teachings and principles. This quest for knowledge aids in personal growth and fosters a stronger connection with the divine.

The ideal human with a strong relationship with God possesses faith, trust, devotion, moral and ethical living, humility, gratitude, service to others, and a thirst for knowledge and understanding. These qualities create a solid foundation for a meaningful and fulfilling relationship with God. Striving to embody these characteristics enables you to unleash your superpower and live a life aligned with your spiritual beliefs while positively impacting the world around you.

Now that we have explored the key characteristics and qualities that an ideal human with a strong relationship with God should possess, let's look at the checklist I have created to help you assess and cultivate these qualities in your own life.

- Nurture your faith and trust in God by regularly reflecting on His existence, power, and guidance. Engage in consistent acts of devotion and worship, such as daily prayer, attending religious services, and engaging in personal spiritual practices.

- Practice moral and ethical living by cultivating qualities such as honesty, integrity, compassion, forgiveness, and love towards others.

- Cultivate and practice humility by recognizing that you are a creation of a higher power and by being open to learning and growing in your relationship with God.

- Have an attitude of gratitude towards God for all blessings, both big and small, and express gratitude through prayers, actions, and a positive mindset.
- Serve others and make a positive impact on the world by engaging in acts of kindness, giving to those in need, and showing compassion towards others.
- Pursue knowledge and understanding of your faith through reading religious texts and seeking guidance from knowledgeable individuals.
- Continuously strive towards embodying the characteristics and qualities mentioned above, recognizing that it is a lifelong journey of growth and improvement.
- Regularly evaluate and assess your relationship with God, adjusting and seeking guidance as needed to deepen and strengthen your connection.
- Seek a community of like-minded individuals who can provide support, guidance, and encouragement in your journey toward a strong relationship with God.

Let's explore some examples that demonstrate how these action steps can be put into practice.

Faith and Trust

You experienced numerous setbacks in life but maintain unwavering faith in God's plan and trust that everything happens for a reason.

You face a challenging decision and seek guidance from God through prayer, trusting that the right path will be revealed to you.

Devotion and Worship

You wake up early every morning to spend time in prayer and meditation, prioritizing your relationship with God above all else.

You actively participate in your religious community, attending religious services regularly, and engaging in rituals and ceremonies with reverence and dedication.

Moral and Ethical Living

You consistently act with integrity and honesty, even when faced with temptations or opportunities to stray from your ethical principles.

You seek ways to help others and exhibit compassion and forgiveness towards those who have wronged you.

Humility

You recognize your talents and accomplishments as gifts from God, remaining humble and acknowledging that they are merely a vessel for God's work.

You readily admit your mistakes and shortcomings, recognizing that you are fallible and in need of God's forgiveness and guidance.

Gratitude

You regularly express gratitude towards God for the blessings in your life, whether big or small, and acknowledge that everything you have is a gift.

You maintain a positive mindset even in difficult times, focusing on the blessings you do have rather than dwelling on what you lack.

Service to Others

You volunteer your time and resources to help those less fortunate, engaging in charitable acts and spreading kindness and love in your community.

You use your skills and talents to make a positive impact in the world, dedicating your life's work to serving others and bringing about positive change.

Seeking Knowledge and Understanding

You actively study your religious texts, attend seminars or workshops and engage in discussions with religious leaders to deepen your understanding of your faith.

You seek guidance and insight from spiritual mentors or leaders to gain a broader perspective on your own beliefs and to grow in your relationship with God.

These examples highlight how individuals with a strong relationship with God embody the characteristics and qualities discussed. Each example showcases a different aspect of what it means to maintain a deep spiritual connection and live a life guided by religious values.

Ruth, a 30-year-old woman, embarked on a personal journey to strengthen her relationship with God and become the ideal human. She recognized the importance of faith, spirituality, and religious values in her life and wanted to cultivate the key characteristics and qualities required to deepen her connection with the divine.

Actions and Initiatives Implemented

1. **Faith and Trust:** Ruth started by developing unwavering faith and trust in God. She engaged in daily prayer and meditation, reflecting on God's power and guidance in her life. Ruth surrendered her worries and fears to God, believing that He had a plan for her.
2. **Devotion and Worship:** Ruth committed to consistent acts of worship, attending religious services regularly, and engaging in personal spiritual practices. She dedicated specific times during the day to praying and reading religious texts, strengthening her bond with God.
3. **Moral and Ethical Living:** Ruth embraced moral and ethical principles in her daily life. She practiced honesty, integrity, compassion, forgiveness, and love toward others, striving to lead a righteous and virtuous life.
4. **Humility:** Ruth cultivated humility by acknowledging that she was a creation of a higher power. She recognized her accomplishments as gifts from God, remaining grounded and open to learning and guidance from Him.

5. **Gratitude:** Ruth adopted an attitude of gratitude, expressing appreciation for God's blessings. She regularly gave thanks through prayers and actively sought to maintain a positive mindset, recognizing the divine presence in her life.

6. **Service to Others:** Ruth engaged in acts of kindness and sought to make a positive impact on others. She volunteered at a local shelter, helped her neighbors in need, and showed compassion towards others, reflecting her love for God through selfless acts.

7. **Seeking Knowledge and Understanding:** Ruth pursued knowledge and understanding of her faith. She read her Bible, and sought guidance from wise individuals, deepening her understanding of God's teachings and principles.

Measurable Outcomes Achieved

Ruth experienced a profound sense of peace and contentment, feeling a stronger connection with God. Ruth witnessed personal growth, becoming more compassionate, forgiving, and loving towards others. Ruth's acts of service positively impacted the lives of those she helped, spreading kindness and love in her community.

Through her quest for knowledge and understanding, Ruth gained a deeper understanding of her faith and felt more spiritually fulfilled.

Challenges Faced

Ruth struggled with doubts and uncertainties at times, particularly when faced with adversity. However, she persisted in her faith, seeking solace in her relationship with God. Balancing her spiritual practices with her responsibilities and commitments proved challenging for Ruth. However, she found ways to prioritize her relationship with God and integrate her faith into her daily life.

Lessons Learned

Ruth learned the significance of persistence and unwavering faith in maintaining a strong relationship with God, even in the face of challenges and doubts.

She realized the transformative power of acts of service and their ability to deepen one's connection with God and positively impact the lives of others.

Ruth understood the importance of humility and gratitude in fostering a relationship with God and maintaining a positive mindset.

Overall Assessment of Impact on Becoming the Ideal Human

Ruth's journey towards becoming the ideal human with a strong relationship with God had a profound impact on her life.

She developed a deeper sense of faith, trust, devotion, moral living, humility, gratitude, service to others, and a thirst for knowledge.

These qualities transformed her perspective, strengthened her bond with the divine, and enabled her to make a positive impact on the world around her.

Ruth's unwavering commitment to becoming the ideal human empowered her to live a life aligned with her spiritual beliefs and values.

Typical Mistakes and How to Avoid Them

1. **Lack of faith and trust:** You struggle to believe in the existence of God or doubt His power and guidance. To avoid this mistake, it is important to cultivate unwavering faith and trust in the divine. **Inconsistent devotion and worship:** You may neglect your spiritual practices, leading to a weak connection with God. Consistency in prayer, attending religious services, and engaging in personal spiritual practices are crucial for building a strong relationship with God.
2. **Moral and ethical shortcomings:** Failing to uphold moral and ethical principles can hinder your relationship with God. It is important to strive for qualities such as honesty, integrity, compassion, forgiveness, and love toward others to maintain a strong connection with the divine.
3. **Lack of humility:** Arrogance and a sense of superiority can alienate you from God. Recognizing your place in creation and being open to learning and guidance from God is essential for a strong

relationship.

Neglecting gratitude: Failing to express gratitude towards God for blessings can weaken the bond with the divine. Cultivating an attitude of gratitude through prayers, actions, and a positive mindset is important for maintaining a strong relationship with God.

4. **Lack of service to others:** Not actively engaging in acts of kindness and selflessly serving others can hinder a strong relationship with God. Demonstrating love for God through compassionate actions is key.

5. **Lack of seeking knowledge and understanding:** Neglecting to pursue knowledge and understanding of your faith can limit the growth of a relationship with God. Engaging in religious study, seeking guidance from knowledgeable individuals, and deepening your understanding of God's teachings is crucial.

To avoid these mistakes, you should strive to cultivate faith and trust, maintain consistent devotion and worship, uphold moral and ethical values, practice humility, express gratitude, engage in acts of service, and actively seek knowledge and understanding of your faith.

My #1 Piece Of Advice

Practice self-compassion and prioritize self-care to promote holistic well-being and personal growth.

Summary

- Unwavering faith and trust in the divine

- Demonstrating devotion and consistent acts of worship

- Living a life by moral and ethical principles

- Embracing humility and acknowledging the guidance of a higher power

- Cultivating an attitude of gratitude and serving others

Quiz

1. What is the foundation for a strong relationship with God?

    A. Faith and trust

    B. Devotion and worship

    C. Moral and ethical living

    D. Humility

2. What is an essential characteristic of individuals with a strong relationship with God?

    A. Honesty

    B. Integrity

    C. Humility

    D. Forgiveness

3. What action is necessary for expressing gratitude towards God?

    A. Prayers

    B. Attending religious services

    C. Engaging in personal spiritual practices

    D. All of the above

4. What is an important quality of an ideal human with a strong relationship with God?

    A. Service to others

    B. Seeking knowledge and understanding

C. Gratitude

D. All of the above

5. What should an individual strive towards to live a life aligned with their spiritual beliefs?

A. Faith and trust

B. Devotion and worship

C. Moral and ethical living

D. Embodying the characteristics outlined in the material

Answer Key

1. A. Faith and trust

2. C. Humility

3. D. All of the above

4. D. All of the above

5. D. Embodying the characteristics outlined in the material

As we explore the definition of an ideal human with a strong relationship with God, it is important to look into the role that emotional intelligence plays in this journey, and how it can be cultivated to enhance our connection with the Divine.

In the following chapter, we will discover the profound impact of emotional intelligence and learn practical ways to develop and nurture this invaluable quality within ourselves.

So, grab a cup of tea, get comfortable, and let's continue this enlightening journey together.

CHAPTER FOUR

Emotional Intelligence: *The Key to Becoming Your Best Self with a Strong Relationship with God*

"Emotional intelligence is the key to unlocking a deep and meaningful relationship with God."

Emotional intelligence plays a crucial role in becoming an ideal human with a strong relationship with God.

Emotional intelligence refers to the ability to recognize, understand, and manage your own emotions, as well as the emotions of others. It allows you to navigate your emotional landscape effectively, making wise decisions and cultivating meaningful connections with others.

Emotional intelligence is particularly relevant in the context of spirituality and the pursuit of a strong relationship with God. Recognizing and understanding your own emotions enables you to develop self-awareness, which is a fundamental aspect of spiritual growth. By becoming aware of your emotional states, you can identify how they may influence your thoughts, behaviors, and ultimately, your connection with a higher power.

Emotional intelligence allows you to empathize with others, which is essential for building and maintaining strong relationships. Empathy not only deepens your understanding of others' experiences but also strengthens your bond with those who share your spiritual journey. Through empathy, you can offer support, compassion, and understanding, fostering an atmosphere of love and unity within your spiritual community.

Developing Emotional Intelligence

2. **Self-reflection:** Start by examining your own emotions and identifying patterns in your behavior. Reflect on how you react in different situations and the impact it has on your relationships. This self-awareness is the first step towards developing emotional intelligence.

3. **Emotional regulation:** Learn to manage and control your emotions. Practice techniques such as deep breathing, mindfulness, and meditation to help you stay calm and composed in challenging situations. This allows you to respond rather than react impulsively, promoting healthier interactions with others.

4. **Empathy development:** Cultivate empathy by actively seeking to understand others' perspectives. Practice active listening, put yourself in their shoes, and strive to validate their emotions. This empathetic approach fosters closer connections within your spiritual community.

5. **Social awareness:** Pay attention to the emotional cues and needs of those around you. Develop the ability to read non-verbal signals and respond appropriately. This helps you establish a deeper connection with others and fosters a more harmonious spiritual environment.

6. **Relationship building:** Invest time and effort in building strong relationships with others who share your spiritual journey. Engage in meaningful conversations, practice active listening, and demonstrate care and support for others' emotional well-being. This allows for a reciprocal exchange of emotions and fosters a deeper relationship with God.

Emotional intelligence plays a significant role in becoming an ideal human with a strong relationship with God. Developing emotional intelligence involves self-reflection, emotional regulation, empathy development, social awareness, and relationship building.

By focusing on these aspects, you can cultivate emotional intelligence and strengthen your connection with God while creating a supportive and nurturing spiritual community. I have created a checklist that outlines the steps you can take to enhance your emotional intelligence.

By following these steps, you can cultivate emotional intelligence and ultimately strengthen your connection with a higher power while fostering a supportive and nurturing spiritual community.

1. **Self-reflection:** Start by examining your own emotions and identifying patterns in your behavior. **Emotional regulation:** Learn techniques such as deep breathing, mindfulness, and meditation to manage and control your emotions.

2. **Empathy development:** Actively seek to understand others' perspectives through active listening and putting yourself in their shoes.

3. **Social awareness:** Pay attention to the emotional cues and needs of those around you and develop the ability to read non-verbal signals.

4. **Relationship building:** Invest time and effort in building strong relationships with others who share your spiritual journey.

How These Strategies Can Be Applied in Practical Situations

1. **Self-reflection:** Reflecting on your emotions and recognizing that you tend to get angry easily when faced with criticism. By reflecting on this pattern, you can begin to identify how it may be affecting your relationship with God and develop strategies to respond differently in those situations.

   Take time to reflect on your emotions during prayer or meditation. This self-awareness can help you better understand how different emotions arise during your spiritual practice and how they may impact your connection with God.

2. **Emotional regulation:** Practicing deep breathing and mindfulness when you feel overwhelmed by stress or anxiety. By regulating your emotions in this way, you can create a calmer and more focused mindset for connecting with God.

3. Choosing not to let negative emotions fuel conflicts within your spiritual community. Instead, you regulate your emotions and respond with understanding and patience, promoting a more harmonious environment.

4. **Empathy development:** Listening attentively to a fellow member of your spiritual community as they share their struggles. By actively seeking to understand their perspective, you can offer support and empathy, strengthening your bond and creating a more compassionate community. Putting yourself in the shoes of someone with a different spiritual background or belief system. Through empathy, you can gain a deeper understanding of their journey and foster mutual respect and understanding.

5. **Social awareness:** Noticing the body language and facial expressions of a friend during a spiritual gathering, recognizing that they may be feeling sad or distant. This social awareness allows you to approach them with care and compassion, providing them with the support they need at that moment. Paying attention to the emotional dynamics within your spiritual community, recognizing when conflicts or tensions arise, and taking steps to address them with sensitivity and understanding.

6. **Relationship building:** Engaging in meaningful conversations with fellow believers, asking about their spiritual experiences and challenges. By building strong relationships based on mutual understanding and support, you can create a network of individuals who uplift and inspire each other.

   Offering emotional support and encouragement to those going through difficult times within your spiritual community. By demonstrating care and compassion, you strengthen your relationships and contribute to a nurturing environment.

You can see how emotional intelligence plays a crucial role in enhancing your relationship with God and creating a nurturing and supportive spiritual community.

Developing Emotional Intelligence and Strengthening a Spiritual Community

The members of a religious community were facing challenges in developing and maintaining strong relationships with each other and with God. There was a lack of understanding and empathy, resulting in conflicts and a sense of disunity within the community. The community leader recognized the importance of emotional intelligence in fostering a strong spiritual connection and decided to implement initiatives to address this issue.

Actions and Initiatives Implemented

1. **Self-reflection workshops:** The community leader organized workshops focused on self-reflection, where members were encouraged to examine their own emotions and behaviors. They were guided through exercises to identify patterns and triggers that influenced their interactions with others and their relationship with God.

2. **Emotional regulation training:** Emotional regulation training sessions were conducted to help members learn techniques such as deep breathing, mindfulness, and meditation. These techniques enabled them to manage their emotions and respond rather than react impulsively, allowing for more constructive and empathetic interactions.

3. **Empathy-building activities:** The community organized activities and discussions aimed at cultivating empathy. Members were encouraged to actively listen to each other, share personal experiences, and practice putting themselves in each other's shoes. This helped them develop a deeper understanding of others' perspectives and validate their emotions.

4. **Non-verbal communication workshops:** Workshops were held to improve social awareness by teaching members to read and respond to non-verbal emotional cues. They learned to pay attention to body language, facial expressions, and tone of voice, which facilitated better understanding and connection with others.

5. **Community-building events:** Regular community-building events were organized, providing opportunities for members to engage in meaningful conversations and develop closer relationships. These events included group discussions, group prayers, and community service activities, emphasizing the importance of care and support for each other's emotional well-being.

Measurable Outcomes Achieved

1. **Increased self-awareness:** Members reported a greater understanding of their own emotions and how they influenced their thoughts, behaviors, and relationship with God.

2. **Improved interpersonal relationships:** Conflict incidents decreased, and members reported feeling more connected and supported by each other. They were able to empathize with and validate each other's emotions, creating a sense of unity within the community.

3. **Deeper spiritual connection:** Members expressed feeling a stronger connection with God as they gained a better understanding of their own emotions and developed empathy for others. They felt more supported and understood in their spiritual journey.

Challenges Faced

1. **Resistance to change:** Some community members initially resisted the implementation of emotional intelligence initiatives, viewing them as unnecessary or unrelated to their spiritual growth.

2. **Sustaining the initiatives:** Maintaining enthusiasm and participation in the emotional intelligence initiatives required ongoing effort and reinforcement from the community leader.

3. **Limited resources:** The community had limited resources, which made it challenging to organize regular workshops and events to support emotional intelligence development.

Lessons Learned

Emotional intelligence is crucial for nurturing a strong spiritual community and deepening one's relationship with God. Developing emotional intelligence requires continuous effort and practice. Effective leadership and consistent reinforcement are essential for sustaining emotional intelligence initiatives.

Collaboration and open communication within the community are necessary to overcome resistance to change and create a supportive environment.

Limited resources can be overcome by leveraging the strengths and talents of community members, such as inviting volunteers to facilitate workshops or organizing low-cost community-building activities.

Overall Assessment of Impact

The implementation of emotional intelligence initiatives had a positive impact on the community's overall emotional well-being and spiritual growth. The members developed self-awareness, empathy, and social awareness, leading to improved relationships and a deeper connection with God. While challenges were faced, the lessons learned highlighted the importance of emotional intelligence in a spiritual context and provided the foundation for ongoing development and growth within the community.

Typical Mistakes and How to Avoid Them

1. **Lack of self-reflection:** You fail to examine your own emotions and behavior patterns, which hinders the development of self-awareness and emotional intelligence. This can lead to unconscious reactions and hinder spiritual growth.

2. **Poor emotional regulation:** You struggle to manage your emotions effectively, resulting in impulsive reactions and strained relationships. Developing techniques for emotional regulation, such as deep breathing and mindfulness, can help avoid these mistakes.

3. **Lack of empathy:** You fail to actively seek to understand others' perspectives and validate their emotions. This can lead to a lack of meaningful connections and a lack of support within a spiritual community.

4. **Limited social awareness:** Not paying attention to the emotional cues and needs of others can hinder the development of deeper connections and harmonious relationships. Developing the ability to read non-verbal signals appropriately is crucial.

5. **Neglecting relationship building:** You fail to invest time and effort in building strong relationships within your spiritual community. Engaging in meaningful conversations and demonstrating care and support for others' emotional well-being is essential for deepening relationships with both others and God.

My #1 Piece Of Advice

My single biggest piece of advice for learning how to control your emotions is to practice self-awareness. Take the time to understand your thoughts, feelings, and triggers. By being aware of your emotions, you can start to identify patterns and begin to respond to them more effectively.

Summary

- Recognize and understand your own emotions to develop self-awareness and spiritual growth.
- Cultivate empathy to deepen your understanding of others and strengthen your bonds with those on their spiritual journey.
- Practice self-reflection and emotional regulation to manage and control your emotions in challenging situations.
- Pay attention to the emotional cues and needs of others to establish deeper connections and create a harmonious spiritual environment.
- Invest time and effort in building strong relationships with others who share your spiritual journey, fostering a deeper connection with God.

Quiz

1. What is emotional intelligence?
A. The ability to recognize, understand, and manage our own emotions
B. The ability to recognize, understand, and manage the emotions of others

C. The ability to navigate our emotional landscape effectively
D. All of the above

2. What is the importance of emotional intelligence in the context of spirituality?
A. It allows individuals to make wise decisions
B. It allows individuals to cultivate meaningful connections with others
C. It enables us to develop self-awareness
D. All of the above

3. What are some steps one can take to develop emotional intelligence?
A. Self-reflection
B. Emotional regulation
C. Empathy development
D. All of the above

4. What is the first step towards developing emotional intelligence?
A. Self-reflection
B. Emotional regulation
C. Empathy development
D. Social awareness

5. What is the purpose of cultivating empathy?
A. To deepen our understanding of others' experiences
B. To strengthen our bonds with those who share our spiritual journey
C. To offer support, compassion, and understanding
D. All of the above

Answer Key

1. D. All of the above
2. D. All of the above
3. D. All of the above
4. A. Self-reflection
5. D. All of the above

You've just discovered the important role emotional intelligence plays in nurturing a strong relationship with God.
Now, let's leap into another crucial aspect of our well-being: our physical health and vitality, and how it can further support our overall well-being and spiritual growth.
So, keep turning the pages, as we explore ways to enhance our vitality and embrace a wholesome life."

CHAPTER FIVE

Igniting Your Inner Fire: *Elevating Physical Health to Support Overall Well-Being and Spiritual Growth*

"Physical health and spiritual growth are not separate entities; they are intertwined, each supporting and enhancing the other." - Unknown

You can enhance your physical health and vitality to support your overall well-being and spiritual growth through a combination of healthy lifestyle choices. The connection between physical health, overall well-being, and spiritual growth has been acknowledged throughout history. It is imperative to prioritize regular exercise as a foundational component of physical health and vitality.

Engaging in moderate to vigorous physical activity not only improves cardiovascular fitness, but also helps maintain a healthy weight, strengthens muscles, and bones, and promotes mental well-being. According to the World Health Organization (WHO), adults should aim for at least 150 minutes of moderate-intensity aerobic activity, or 75 minutes of vigorous-intensity aerobic activity, per week.

Additionally, muscle-strengthening activities, such as weightlifting, should be performed at least twice a week. By adhering to these guidelines, individuals can elevate their physical well-being and enhance their overall vitality. A balanced and nutritious diet is paramount in supporting physical health and providing the body with the energy and nutrients it needs for optimal functioning. A diet rich in whole foods, including fruits, vegetables, whole grains, lean proteins, and healthy fats, is essential. Research has consistently shown that such a diet can reduce the risk of chronic diseases, maintain a healthy weight, and promote longevity.

Additionally, staying adequately hydrated by consuming an appropriate amount of water throughout the day is crucial for optimal physical performance. Sufficient rest and sleep are often overlooked but are equally important for physical health and vitality. Sleep allows the body to repair and regenerate, supports cognitive function, and balances hormonal levels.

The National Sleep Foundation recommends that adults aim for 6-8 hours of quality sleep per night. Establishing a consistent sleep routine, creating a conducive sleep environment, and practicing relaxation techniques before bed can greatly aid in achieving the recommended sleep duration.

Managing stress is imperative for physical health, overall well-being, and spiritual growth. Chronic stress can have detrimental effects on the body, including increased inflammation, compromised immune system function, and heightened risk of various health conditions. Engaging in stress-reducing activities such as mindfulness meditation, deep breathing exercises, or engaging in hobbies can effectively alleviate stress and promote a healthier and more balanced life. It is important to highlight the significance of preventive healthcare measures.

Regular medical check-ups, screenings, and vaccinations can help detect and prevent potential health issues before they become more serious. You should establish a trusted relationship with a primary care physician who can provide guidance and counsel based on your specific needs. Enhancing physical health and vitality to support overall well-being and spiritual growth requires a comprehensive approach.

By incorporating regular exercise, a balanced and nutritious diet, adequate rest and sleep, stress management techniques, and preventive healthcare measures, individuals can optimize their physical health and lay the foundation for spiritual growth. It is crucial to approach these recommendations with determination, attention to detail, and a commitment to following established procedures to achieve desired results. With deliberate action and unwavering commitment, individuals can attain divine physical health and unlock their fullest potential for well-being and spiritual growth.

Now that we have explored strategies and practices for enhancing physical health and vitality, let's dive into a checklist that can be used as a practical guide to implementing these recommendations in your daily life.

1. **Regular Exercise:** Aim for at least 150 minutes of moderate-intensity aerobic activity or 75 minutes of vigorous-intensity aerobic activity per week. Engage in muscle-strengthening activities at least twice a week. Consider activities like weightlifting or other forms of exercise that suit your preferences and abilities.

2. **Balanced and Nutritious Diet:** Emphasize whole foods such as fruits, vegetables, whole grains, lean proteins, and healthy fats. Reduce processed and sugary foods in your diet. Stay adequately hydrated by consuming an appropriate amount of water throughout the day.

3. **Sufficient Rest and Sleep:** Aim for 7-9 hours of quality sleep per night. Establish a consistent sleep routine and create a conducive sleep environment. Practice relaxation techniques before bedtime, such as deep breathing exercises or meditation.

4. **Stress Management:** Engage in stress-reducing activities such as mindfulness meditation, deep breathing exercises, or engaging in hobbies. Identify and address sources of stress in your life. Prioritize self-care and set aside time for relaxation and activities that bring you joy.

5. **Preventive Healthcare Measures:** Schedule regular medical check-ups and screenings. Stay up-to-date with vaccinations recommended by healthcare professionals. Establish a trusted relationship with a primary care physician who can provide guidance and counsel based on your specific needs.

By following these action steps, you can enhance your physical health and vitality, support your overall well-being, and lay the foundation for spiritual growth.

Putting The Steps Into Action

1. **Regular exercise:** Incorporate 30 minutes of jogging and 20 minutes of weightlifting into your daily routine.

   Balanced and nutritious diet: Adopt a plant-based diet, focusing on consuming a variety of fruits, vegetables, legumes, and whole grains.

2. **Sufficient rest and sleep:** Establish a consistent sleep routine and get 6-8 hours of quality sleep every night.

3. **Stress management techniques:** Practice mindfulness meditation for 10 minutes every morning and evening.

4. **Preventive healthcare measures:** Visit your primary care physician regularly for check-ups and screenings.

By putting these steps into action, you can experience firsthand the connection between physical health, overall well-being, and spiritual growth.

Cultivating Divine Physical Health for Well-Being and Spiritual Growth

John is a 45-year-old male who has been feeling physically lethargic and spiritually disconnected for the past year. He has a sedentary lifestyle and often relies on fast food for his meals. John has recognized the importance of physical health in supporting his well-being and spiritual growth and is motivated to make positive changes in his life.

Key Actions and Initiatives Implemented

1. **Regular Exercise:** John started by incorporating a regular exercise routine into his daily life. He committed to exercising for at least 30 minutes every day, combining both aerobic activities like jogging and strength-training exercises like weightlifting. He began with moderate-intensity workouts and gradually increased the intensity as his fitness level improved.

2. **Balanced and Nutritious Diet:** John made significant changes to his diet, focusing on consuming whole foods and eliminating processed foods. He incorporated a variety of fruits, vegetables, whole grains, lean proteins, and healthy fats into his meals. John learned about portion control and started preparing his meals to have better control over the ingredients he used.

3. **Sufficient Rest and Sleep:** John recognized the importance of adequate rest and sleep. He established a consistent sleep routine, going to bed and waking up at the same time every day. He created a calm and comfortable sleep environment in his bedroom and practiced relaxation techniques like meditation and deep breathing before bedtime to improve the quality of his sleep.

4. **Stress Management Techniques:** To manage stress, John started practicing mindfulness meditation and engaging in deep breathing exercises regularly. Additionally, he prioritized engaging in hobbies and activities that brought him joy and relaxation, such as gardening and painting.

5. **Preventive Healthcare Measures:** John scheduled an appointment with a primary care physician for a comprehensive medical check-up. Based on the doctor's recommendations, he received necessary screenings and vaccinations to prevent potential health issues.

Measurable Outcomes Achieved

John's fitness level significantly improved, as evidenced by increased stamina, strength, and flexibility. John lost 15 pounds over six months and maintained a healthy weight. John's blood pressure, cholesterol levels, and other health markers improved, reducing his risk of chronic diseases. John reported feeling more energized, mentally clear, and spiritually connected. John achieved an overall sense of well-being, experiencing lower levels of stress and improved happiness.

Challenges Faced

John faced difficulty adjusting to a more active lifestyle and healthier eating habits. He experienced muscle soreness and cravings for unhealthy foods. However, with perseverance and support from a wellness coach, he overcame these challenges. Finding time for exercise and meal preparation within his busy schedule was another obstacle. John had to prioritize his well-being over other commitments and make conscious efforts to manage his time effectively.

Lessons Learned

John realized the importance of starting small and gradually increasing the intensity and complexity of his lifestyle changes. He experienced firsthand the impact of consistent practice and perseverance in achieving physical and spiritual growth. John discovered the value of seeking support and guidance from professionals, such as wellness coaches and healthcare providers, to stay motivated and accountable.

Overall Assessment of Impact on Physical Health

Through a comprehensive approach to enhancing physical health, John successfully improved his overall well-being and spiritual growth. The combination of regular exercise, a balanced diet, sufficient rest, stress management techniques, and preventive healthcare measures profoundly impacted his physical health. John's increased fitness, weight loss, improved health markers, and enhanced energy levels demonstrate the effectiveness of these strategies.

By adopting a holistic approach, John experienced a positive shift in his mental and spiritual well-being, enabling him to lead a more fulfilling and connected life.

Typical Mistakes And How To Avoid Them

1. **Neglecting regular exercise:** Prioritizing regular exercise is essential for physical health and vitality. Failure to engage in moderate to vigorous physical activity can lead to poor cardiovascular fitness, weight gain, and overall decline in health. Regular exercise should be a foundational component of a healthy lifestyle.

2. **Unhealthy eating habits:** Following an unhealthy diet that lacks essential nutrients and is high in processed foods. Emphasizing a balanced and nutritious diet, rich in whole foods such as fruits, vegetables, whole grains, lean proteins, and healthy fats, is crucial for maintaining physical health and providing the body with the necessary energy and nutrients.

3. **Inadequate rest and sleep:** Sufficient rest and sleep are often overlooked, but they play a vital role in physical health and vitality. Lack of sleep can lead to impaired cognitive function, hormonal imbalances, and increased risk of health conditions. Establishing a consistent sleep routine and practicing relaxation techniques before bed can greatly improve sleep quality.

4. **Neglecting stress management:** Chronic stress can have detrimental effects on physical health and overall well-being. Many individuals fail to prioritize stress management techniques such as mindfulness meditation, deep breathing exercises, and engaging in hobbies. Managing stress is crucial for maintaining optimal physical health and promoting spiritual growth.

5. **Lack of preventive healthcare measures:** Regular medical check-ups, screenings, and vaccinations are essential for detecting and preventing potential health issues. Many people neglect these preventive measures, which can lead to undetected health problems. Establishing a trusted relationship with a primary care physician is important for receiving proper guidance and counsel.

To avoid these mistakes, you should prioritize regular exercise, maintain a balanced and nutritious diet, ensure sufficient rest and sleep, practice stress management techniques, and follow preventive healthcare measures.

By approaching these recommendations with determination, attention to detail, and committing to established procedures, you can enhance your physical health and vitality, supporting your overall well-being and spiritual growth.

My #1 Piece Of Advice

Take care of your physical health by prioritizing quality sleep, regular exercise, nourishing food, and proper hydration.

Summary

- Prioritize regular exercise as a foundational component of physical health and vitality to improve cardiovascular fitness, maintain a healthy weight, strengthen muscles and bones, and promote mental well-being.

- Emphasize a balanced and nutritious diet, rich in whole foods to reduce the risk of chronic diseases, maintain a healthy weight, and promote longevity.

- Ensure sufficient rest and sleep by aiming for 6-8 hours of quality sleep per night to support body repair, cognitive function, and hormonal balance.

- Manage stress levels through stress-reducing activities such as mindfulness meditation, deep breathing exercises, or engaging in hobbies to alleviate stress and promote a healthier and more balanced life.

- Prioritize preventive healthcare measures, such as regular medical check-ups, screenings, and vaccinations, to detect and prevent potential health issues before they become more serious.

Quiz

1. What is the recommended amount of aerobic activity for adults per week according to the World Health Organization (WHO)?
A. 30 minutes
B. 60 minutes
C. 90 minutes

D. 150 minutes

2. Which of the following are recommended components of a balanced and nutritious diet?
A. Fruits
B. Vegetables
C. Whole grains
D. Lean proteins
E. Healthy fats

3. What is the recommended amount of sleep for adults per night according to the National Sleep Foundation?
A. 4-6 hours
B. 6-8 hours
C. 7-9 hours
D. 9-10 hours

4. What is the primary goal of preventive healthcare measures?
A. To detect and prevent health issues
B. To provide guidance and counsel
C. To manage stress levels
D. To promote longevity

5. What is the importance of managing stress levels for physical health, overall well-being, and spiritual growth?
A. It can reduce inflammation
B. It can improve cognitive function
C. It can enhance the immune system
D. It can increase the risk of chronic diseases

Answer Key

1. D
2. A, B, C, D, E
3. C
4. A
5. A, B, C, D

As we've explored in this chapter, taking care of our physical health is essential for our overall well-being and spiritual growth.

Now, let's probe into the next topic, which is equally crucial: how we can strike a balance between self-care and caring for others, while also nurturing our relationship with God.

CHAPTER SIX

Balancing Self and Service: *Nurturing Well-Being while Cultivating Relationships and Connection with God*

"You cannot pour from an empty cup; prioritize self-care so that you can pour love and care into the lives of others."

Creating a balance between focusing on your well-being and caring for others while maintaining a strong relationship with God is indeed a complex task. However, with careful consideration and a conscious effort, you can achieve this balance by following a few key principles.

First and foremost, you must recognize the importance of self-care. To effectively care for others, you must ensure your well-being is prioritized. This includes taking care of physical, emotional, and mental health. Engaging in activities that promote self-care, such as regular exercise, adequate sleep, and mindfulness practices, allows you to recharge and replenish your energy. By investing in your well-being, you become better equipped to care for others in a more sustainable and meaningful way.

Simultaneously, maintaining a strong relationship with God can provide you with the spiritual and emotional support needed to navigate the challenges of caring for others while also tending to your own needs. Engaging in regular prayer, meditation, or religious practices can offer solace, guidance, and a sense of connection with a higher power. This connection can serve as a source of strength and resilience during times of difficulty or when faced with the demands of caring for others.

Additionally, setting clear boundaries is crucial when striving to strike a balance between self-care and caring for others. It is important to recognize that it is not selfish to prioritize personal well-being and that saying "no" or taking time for oneself is essential for overall well-being. Establishing boundaries in relationships and establishing realistic expectations about what one can or cannot do when it comes to caring for others is key.

Communicating these boundaries clearly and respectfully can help ensure that both self-care and caring for others can coexist harmoniously. Moreover, you can utilize support systems to distribute the responsibility of caring for others while still prioritizing your well-being. This can include seeking assistance from friends, family, or community resources to share the burden of care. By fostering a network of support, you can delegate tasks and responsibilities, enabling you to meet your own needs while still fulfilling your commitment to caring for others.

Creating a balance between focusing on personal well-being and caring for others requires you to prioritize self-care, establish boundaries, engage in spiritual practices, and foster a support system. By adhering to these principles, you can effectively meet your own needs without neglecting your responsibility to care for others. Now that you have read about the importance of balancing self-care, caring for others, and maintaining a strong relationship with God, I have created a checklist to help you implement these principles in your life.

1. **Prioritize self-care:** Engage in regular exercise, adequate sleep, and mindfulness practices to replenish energy and promote physical, emotional, and mental well-being.
2. **Maintain a strong relationship with God:** Engage in regular prayer, meditation, or religious practices to seek spiritual and emotional support and guidance.
3. **Set clear boundaries:** Recognize that it is not selfish to prioritize personal well-being and establish realistic expectations about what you can or cannot do when it comes to caring for others. Communicate these boundaries clearly and respectfully.
4. **Utilize support systems:** Seek assistance from friends, family, or community resources to share the responsibility of caring for others. Delegate tasks and responsibilities to meet your own needs while fulfilling your commitment to caring for others.

By following these action steps, you can effectively create a balance between focusing on self-care and caring for others while maintaining a strong relationship with God.

Now that we have gone through the checklist, let's look at some examples that demonstrate how these steps can be implemented in your life.

- **Jane** is a mother of two young children. She recognizes the importance of self-care and ensures that she sets aside time each day to engage in activities that replenish her energy. She wakes up early to exercise and practices mindfulness during her lunch break. By prioritizing her well-being, Jane finds that she has more patience and energy to devote to her children, making her a more present and engaged mother.

- **John** is a devoted Christian who finds solace and guidance in his daily prayers and religious practices. He works as a nurse and often encounters challenging situations that require him to care for others while still attending to his own needs. John finds that by turning to his faith, he can find strength and resilience during difficult times. His relationship with God provides him with the emotional support he needs to balance caring for others with self-care.

- **Connie** is a college student who is heavily involved in several volunteer organizations. She has a passion for helping others, but often finds herself overwhelmed by the demands of her commitments. Sarah learns how to set boundaries in her relationships by clearly communicating what she can and cannot do. By doing so, she can establish realistic expectations and prevent burnout. This allows her to continue caring for others without sacrificing her well-being.

- **David** is a caregiver for his elderly father, who requires round-the-clock assistance. David realizes that he cannot provide all of the care on his own without neglecting his own needs. He reaches out to his siblings and other family members for support, asking them to share in the responsibility of caring for their father. By creating a support system, David can distribute the burden of care and ensure that he can still prioritize his well-being while fulfilling his commitment to his father.

- **Lisa** is a teacher who often feels drained from the demands of her job and personal life. She decides to incorporate daily meditation into her routine to help restore her energy and maintain her inner peace. Lisa finds that by taking this time for herself, she can approach her work with a renewed sense of clarity and compassion. This allows her to effectively care for her students while still prioritizing her well-being.

Each of these examples demonstrates the importance of self-care in maintaining well-being while fulfilling the responsibilities of caregiving.

Balancing Self-Care, Caring for Others, while Maintaining a Relationship with God in a Healthcare Setting

1. **Importance of Self-Care:** Healthcare professionals in the organization recognize that to effectively care for others, they must prioritize their well-being. They understand that self-care is not selfish but rather essential for sustaining their ability to provide quality care. They engage in various self-care activities such as exercise, adequate sleep, and mindfulness practices to recharge and replenish their energy.

2. **Maintaining a Strong Relationship with God:** Healthcare professionals also understand the importance of maintaining a spiritual connection with God as a source of strength and guidance. They engage in regular prayer, meditation, and religious practices to find solace, support, and a sense of higher purpose. This helps them navigate the challenges they face while caring for others.

3. **Setting Clear Boundaries:** Healthcare professionals establish clear boundaries to strike a balance between self-care and caring for others. They understand that saying "no" or taking time for themselves is not selfish but necessary for their overall well-being. They communicate these boundaries respectfully to ensure that both self-care and caring for others can coexist harmoniously.

4. **Utilizing Support Systems:** Healthcare professionals utilize support systems to distribute the responsibility of caring for others while still prioritizing their well-being. They seek assistance from colleagues, family, and community resources to share the burden of care. This enables them to delegate tasks and responsibilities, ensuring that they can meet their own needs while fulfilling their commitment to caring for others.

Measurable Outcomes

1. **Improved Job Satisfaction:** Healthcare professionals report higher job satisfaction because of prioritizing self-care, setting boundaries, and maintaining a strong relationship with God. They feel more fulfilled in their work and can provide quality care to patients.

2. **Reduced Burnout and Stress Levels:** The implementation of self-care practices and boundary-setting leads to reduced burnout and stress levels among healthcare professionals. They experience improved mental and emotional well-being, enabling them to perform their duties effectively.

Challenges Faced

1. **Balancing Workload:** Healthcare professionals often struggle with balancing their workload and personal life. The demands of caring for others can be overwhelming at times, making it crucial for them to implement effective strategies to manage their responsibilities.
2. **Resisting Guilt:** Some healthcare professionals initially struggle with feelings of guilt when prioritizing self-care or setting boundaries. Overcoming this guilt requires a shift in mindset and recognizing the importance of their well-being to effectively care for others.

Lessons Learned

1. **Self-Care is Essential:** Prioritizing self-care is not only important but necessary for healthcare professionals to provide sustainable and meaningful care to others.
2. **Setting Boundaries is Vital:** Establishing clear boundaries and communicating them effectively is crucial for maintaining a healthy balance between self-care and caring for others.
3. **Utilize Support Systems:** Seeking assistance and relying on support systems help distribute the responsibilities of caring for others, preventing burnout, and ensuring overall well-being.

Overall Assessment of Impact on Empathy

The implementation of self-care, boundary-setting, and maintaining a relationship with God has positively impacted the empathy level of healthcare professionals. By prioritizing their well-being and fostering a support system, they are better equipped to empathize with patients while providing compassionate care.

This ultimately strengthens their connection with patients and enhances the overall quality of care provided by the organization.

Typical Mistakes And How To Avoid Them

A common mistake that most people make in this area is neglecting their well-being while caring for others. This mistake can be avoided by prioritizing self-care and recognizing its importance in effectively helping others.

Another mistake is failing to establish clear boundaries. To avoid this mistake, you should set realistic expectations and communicate your boundaries respectfully.

Finally, another mistake is not utilizing support systems. This can be avoided by seeking assistance from friends, family, or community resources to share caregiving responsibilities.

By following these principles, you can achieve a balance between self-care, caring for others, and maintaining a strong relationship with God.

My #1 Piece Of Advice

Practice active listening and genuine curiosity to understand others' perspectives, feelings, and experiences.

Summary

- **Prioritize self-care:** Recognize the importance of taking care of your own physical, emotional, and mental well-being to effectively care for others. Engage in activities that promote self-care, recharge your energy, and maintain overall health.

- **Maintain a strong relationship with God:** Find solace, guidance, and emotional support through regular prayer, meditation, and religious practices. Cultivate a connection with God to give you strength and resilience when faced with the challenges of caring for others.

- **Set clear boundaries:** Understand that prioritizing personal well-being is not selfish. Establish boundaries in relationships and communicate them clearly and respectfully. Learning to say "no" and take time for yourself is essential for a balanced life.

- **Utilize support systems:** Seek assistance from friends, family, and community resources to share the responsibility of caring for others. By fostering a network of support, you can delegate tasks and responsibilities, allowing you to meet your own needs while fulfilling your commitment to others.

- **Adhere to these principles:** Prioritize self-care, establish boundaries, engage in spiritual practices, and foster a support system. By following these principles, you can effectively meet your own needs without neglecting your responsibility to care for others, all while maintaining a strong connection to your spiritual beliefs.

Quiz

1. What is the primary focus of the material?
   - A. Establishing boundaries
   - B. Caring for others
   - C. Maintaining a strong relationship with God
   - D. Prioritizing self-care

2. What is an example of an activity that promotes self-care?
   - A. Praying
   - B. Watching television
   - C. Exercising
   - D. Working late

3. What is a key principle for achieving a balance between caring for oneself and caring for others?
   - A. Fostering a support system
   - B. Saying "no"
   - C. Setting realistic expectations
   - D. All of the above

4. What does engaging in spiritual practices provide individuals with?
   - A. Emotional support
   - B. Physical strength

C. Financial resources

D. Social connections

5. What can happen if individuals neglect their responsibility to care for others?

A. They can become isolated

B. They can become more financially secure

C. They can become more spiritually connected

D. They can become more physically healthy

Answer Key

1. D
2. C
3. D
4. A
5. A

You have explored the delicate balance between personal well-being and caring for others while nurturing your relationship with God.

It is important to recognize the significance of community and support in your journey towards holistic well-being and spiritual growth.

In the upcoming chapter, we will explore the role that community plays in your life and discover how you can actively engage and build a supportive network.

CHAPTER SEVEN

Together We Rise: *The Impact of Community on Our Journey to Wholeness*

"A single candle can illuminate a room, but a community of candles can ignite a fire that spreads inspiration and sparks positive change."

Community and support play an integral role in your journey towards holistic well-being and spiritual growth. Humans are inherently social beings, and your well-being is deeply influenced by the connections and relationships you form with others. Within a supportive community, you can receive and provide meaningful support, guidance, and encouragement as you pursue your personal growth. The importance of community and support can be observed across various aspects of your life.

From a mental and emotional standpoint, being part of a supportive network provides a space where you can share your experiences, challenges, and thoughts. Open dialogues and discussions within a community help you gain different perspectives, receive valuable feedback, and find solace in the shared struggles and triumphs of others. This connection fosters a sense of belonging, reduces feelings of isolation, and contributes to overall mental well-being.

On a physical level, being part of a community can promote healthy lifestyles and encourage positive habits. When you engage in activities together, such as exercise groups, cooking clubs, or sports teams, you can motivate and hold each other accountable for achieving your wellness goals. The supportive network acts as a foundation for adopting healthy routines, providing motivation, and celebrating achievements. This can have a profound impact on physical well-being, leading to increased energy levels, improved fitness, and reduced stress.

Community and support can positively influence your spiritual growth as you, search for meaning, purpose, and connection to something greater than yourself. Engaging with a supportive network that shares similar spiritual or religious beliefs can provide a sense of unity and purpose. It creates an environment where you can explore your spirituality, engage in meaningful discussions, and find guidance in your faith.

This shared journey toward spiritual growth allows for deep connections, support during challenging times, and an opportunity to learn from others' perspectives and experiences. To engage with and build a supportive network, you can take proactive steps to connect with like-minded individuals. This can include joining community organizations, attending spiritual or religious gatherings, participating in meet-ups or workshops centered around personal growth, or engaging in online communities and forums.

By actively seeking out opportunities for connection, you can meet others who share similar values, interests, and aspirations. Building a supportive network also involves investing time and effort into these relationships. It requires being open and vulnerable with others, actively listening and providing support, and demonstrating a genuine willingness to help and contribute.

Creating a reliable and trusting support system takes time, but the rewards are immense, as it can profoundly impact personal growth, well-being, and spiritual development. Community and support are vital in your journey towards holistic well-being and spiritual growth. By engaging with and building a supportive network, you can access the necessary resources to thrive mentally, emotionally, physically, and spiritually. It provides a safe space for personal exploration, equips you with the tools for achieving wellness goals, and promotes a sense of belonging and purpose.

Therefore, actively seeking and nurturing these connections is crucial for your overall well-being and spiritual development. Let's dive into a checklist that can help you actively seek and nurture the connections that are crucial for your overall well-being and spiritual development.

1. **Connect with like-minded individuals:** Take proactive steps to connect with people who share similar values, interests, and aspirations. This can include joining community organizations, attending spiritual or religious gatherings, participating in meet-ups or workshops centered around personal growth, or engaging in online communities and forums.
2. **Invest in relationships:** Building a supportive network requires time and effort. Be open and vulnerable with others, actively listen and provide support, and demonstrate a genuine willingness to help and contribute. Creating a reliable and trusting support system takes time, but the rewards are immense.

3. **Seek support:** Reach out to others when you need guidance, encouragement, or a listening ear. Seek support from trusted friends, family members, or mentors who can provide valuable feedback and support during challenging times.

4. **Engage in open dialogues and discussions:** Within a supportive community, participate in open dialogues and discussions where you can share your experiences, challenges, and thoughts. Gain different perspectives, receive valuable feedback, and find solace in the shared struggles and triumphs of others.

5. **Engage in activities together:** Participate in activities with your supportive network that promotes healthy lifestyles and positive habits. Join exercise groups, cooking clubs, or sports teams to motivate and hold each other accountable for achieving wellness goals. The supportive network acts as a foundation for adopting healthy routines, providing motivation, and celebrating achievements.

6. **Attend spiritual or religious gatherings:** If you have spiritual or religious beliefs, attend gatherings where you can connect with others who share similar beliefs. Engaging with a supportive network that shares similar beliefs can provide a sense of unity and purpose and create an environment where you can explore your spirituality, engage in meaningful discussions, and find guidance in your faith.

7. **Engage in personal growth activities:** Participate in meet-ups or workshops centered around personal growth and self-improvement. These activities can provide opportunities to connect with like-minded individuals and you can acquire new tools and strategies for personal development.

8. **Take care of your mental and emotional well-being:** Prioritize your mental and emotional well-being by practicing self-care, seeking professional help if needed, and engaging in activities that promote stress reduction and emotional health.

9. **Prioritize physical well-being:** Incorporate healthy habits into your lifestyle, such as regular exercise, a balanced diet, sufficient sleep, and stress reduction. Engage in physical activities with your supportive network to promote accountability and motivation.

10. **Embrace a sense of belonging and purpose:** Cultivate a sense of belonging and purpose within your supportive network by actively participating in activities and discussions, sharing your experiences, and providing support to others. Embrace the connection and unity that comes with being part of a community.

Now that we have gone through the checklist, let's look at some examples that demonstrate how you can apply these principles in your life.

1. **Mental and emotional support:** Imagine a person struggling with depression, feeling isolated and alone. By seeking out a support group and connecting with others who have experienced similar struggles, you can share your experiences, gain different perspectives, and receive valuable guidance and encouragement. This supportive community provides a safe space for you to open up, express your emotions, and find solace in knowing that you are not alone in your journey.

2. **Physical well-being:** Consider a group of friends who decide to start a running club. By regularly meeting up to exercise together, you provide motivation and accountability for each other. You can set goals, track progress, and celebrate each other's achievements. This supportive network not only encourages healthy habits but also creates a sense of camaraderie and teamwork, making the fitness journey more enjoyable and sustainable.

3. **Spiritual growth:** Picture a person exploring their spirituality and seeking guidance in their faith. By joining a religious or spiritual community, you can connect with others who share similar beliefs. This supportive network offers a space for discussing spiritual teachings and engaging in meaningful conversations. Through these interactions, you can deepen your understanding, find support during challenging times, and experience a sense of unity and purpose.

4. **Personal growth workshops:** Imagine attending a personal growth workshop where you can come together to learn and grow. In this setting, you can connect with like-minded individuals who are also on a journey towards self-improvement. The workshop provides a supportive community where you can share your aspirations, learn from each other's experiences, and offer encouragement and motivation. This community setting fosters personal growth by providing a space for reflection, skill-building, and the opportunity to receive guidance from experts and peers.

5. **Online communities and forums:** Consider turning to online communities and forums for support and connection. Whether it's a mental health support group, a wellness platform, or a spiritual discussion forum, these online communities provide a space to connect with others who share similar interests and struggles. Through virtual interactions, you can seek advice, share resources, and offer support to one another. These online communities act as a source of solace, inspiration, and knowledge, contributing to an individual's overall well-being and personal growth.

These examples illustrate how community and support are essential elements in various aspects of your life. By actively engaging with and building a supportive network, you can access the necessary resources to thrive mentally, emotionally, physically, and spiritually.

It is through these connections that personal growth, well-being, and spiritual development can truly flourish. Having explored the importance of community and support in different areas of life, let's now dive into a case study that examines the impact of a supportive network on your personal growth and well-being.

Building a Supportive Community for Spiritual Growth

A local community organization, the Center for Spiritual Development (CSD), recognized the need for a supportive network to assist individuals in their spiritual journeys. They aimed to provide a space where individuals could connect with like-minded individuals, share their experiences, and receive guidance and support.

1. **Establishing the Center for Spiritual Development (CSD):** The CSD was founded as a hub for people seeking spiritual growth and connection. The center offers various programs, workshops, and events that focus on personal exploration and spiritual development.
2. **Monthly Gatherings for Shared Discussion:** CSD organized monthly gatherings where people could come together in a supportive environment and engage in open dialogues and discussions about their spirituality. Topics such as finding meaning, purpose, and connection were explored, providing an opportunity for individuals to gain different perspectives and insights.
3. **Support Groups:** The center facilitated the formation of support groups based on common interests and spiritual beliefs. These groups provided a safe space for individuals to share their challenges and triumphs, ask for guidance, and offer support to one another.
4. **Mentorship Program:** CSD established a mentorship program where more experienced members of the community volunteered to support and guide newcomers on their spiritual journeys. Mentors shared their own experiences, offered resources, and provided encouragement to their mentees.

Measurable Outcomes

1. **Increased Attendance and Engagement:** The center saw a significant increase in the number of people attending its programs, workshops, and events, indicating a growing interest in the community's offerings.
2. **Positive Feedback:** Participants reported feeling a sense of belonging, finding a support system, and experiencing personal growth through their involvement with the community.
3. **Enhanced Spiritual Growth**: Many people reported significant development in their spiritual lives, citing the support they received as a crucial factor in their progress. This included a deeper sense of purpose, improved connection with their spiritual beliefs, and a stronger sense of inner peace and well-being.

Challenges Faced

1. **Building Trust:** It took time to build trust and encourage people to be vulnerable and open in sharing their experiences and challenges. The community had to work on creating an inclusive and non-judgmental environment.
2. **Sustaining Engagement:** Maintaining consistent attendance and engagement proved challenging as people faced competing commitments and demands on their time.
3. **Diverse Beliefs and Perspectives:** The community had to navigate different spiritual beliefs and perspectives, ensuring that all individuals felt respected and included.

Lessons Learned

1. **Patience and Persistence:** Building a supportive community takes time, and cultivating an environment of trust and inclusivity requires ongoing effort and patience.
2. **Genuine Connection:** Authentic and meaningful connections are vital for people to feel supported and experience personal growth.
3. **Flexibility:** The community learned the importance of adapting and offering a diverse range of programs and resources to cater to the varied needs and interests of its members.

4. **Overall Impact on the Community:** The establishment of the Center for Spiritual Development and the creation of a supportive community had a significant impact on the overall well-being and spiritual growth of its members. Individuals found a sense of belonging and purpose, formed deep connections, and experienced personal growth through their involvement. The community provided a valuable support system that positively influenced mental, emotional, physical, and spiritual well-being.

Typical Mistakes And How To Avoid Them

A mistake that most people make in this area is not actively seeking and nurturing connections with a supportive community. This can be avoided by taking proactive steps to connect with like-minded individuals, such as joining community organizations, attending gatherings, participating in workshops, or engaging in online communities and forums.

Another mistake is not investing enough time and effort into building these relationships. Avoid this by being open and vulnerable with others, actively listening and providing support, and demonstrating a genuine willingness to help and contribute. The key to recognizing the importance of community and support in our well-being and spiritual growth is to actively seek and nurture these connections for personal growth and development.

My #1 Piece Of Advice

Seek out and engage in supportive and empathetic relationships to foster healing and well-being.

Summary

- Community and support are essential for holistic well-being and spiritual growth.

- Being part of a supportive network allows for sharing experiences, gaining different perspectives, and finding solace in shared struggles and triumphs.

- Engaging with a community promotes healthy lifestyles and encourages positive habits, leading to increased energy levels and reduced stress.

- A supportive network that shares similar spiritual or religious beliefs provides unity, purpose, and guidance on the journey toward spiritual growth.

- Taking proactive steps to connect with like-minded individuals and investing time and effort into relationships can profoundly impact personal growth, well-being, and spiritual development.

Quiz

1. What is the main point of this material?

A. The importance of community and support
B. How to engage with and build a supportive network
C. The impact of community and support on personal growth
D. How to achieve mental, emotional, physical, and spiritual wellness

2. What does community and support contribute to?
A. Mental and emotional well-being
B. Physical wellness

C. Spiritual growth

D. All of the above

3. What are some proactive steps an individual can take to connect with like-minded people?

A. Joining community organizations

B. Attending spiritual or religious gatherings

C. Participating in meet-ups

D. Engaging in online communities and forums

E. All of the above

4. What is required for building a reliable and trusting support system?

A. Taking time to connect with others

B. Being open and vulnerable with others

C. Actively listening and providing support

D. Demonstrating a genuine willingness to help and contribute

E. All of the above

5. What is the importance of community and support?

A. It creates an environment where individuals can explore their spirituality

B. It helps people gain different perspectives

C. It fosters a sense of belonging and reduces feelings of isolation

D. It provides motivation and accountability toward achieving wellness goals

E. All of the above

Answer Key

1. C

2. D

3. E

4. E

5. E\

As you explore the significance of community and support in your holistic well-being and spiritual growth.

You must also delve into the power of forgiveness in nurturing our mental, emotional, physical, and spiritual health.

In the next chapter, we will delve into the transformative nature of forgiveness and discover practical ways in which you can cultivate this essential virtue within your heart and life.

So, grab a smoothie, and let's explore the profound impact forgiveness can have on your well-being and spiritual evolution.

CHAPTER EIGHT

The Healing Power of Forgiveness: *Transforming Mental, Emotional, Physical, and Spiritual Well-being*

"Don't let the wounds of the past define your future. Embrace forgiveness and empower yourself to heal and grow."

Forgiveness plays a pivotal role in your mental, emotional, physical, and spiritual well-being. Research and various studies have consistently demonstrated the positive impact of forgiveness on your overall health and happiness. When you hold onto anger, resentment, or bitterness, it can profoundly affect your mental and emotional state, which can subsequently manifest as physical ailments. Harboring unforgiveness can hinder your spiritual growth and experience. To cultivate forgiveness in your heart and life, you must follow a structured and intentional approach.

Here Are Some Strategies Proven To Be Effective

1. **Acceptance and Acknowledgment:** The journey towards forgiveness begins by accepting the reality of the hurt or harm suffered. By acknowledging the pain experienced, you can come to terms with your emotions and gradually work towards forgiving the offender.
2. **Empathy and Perspective-Taking:** Empathy plays a significant role in forgiveness. It involves placing yourself in the other person's shoes and striving to understand their motivations, struggles, and potential reasons for their actions. This perspective-taking exercise helps you develop empathy, which can facilitate the forgiveness process.
3. **Emotional Release:** Forgiveness does not require suppressing or denying one's emotions. It encourages you to acknowledge your feelings of anger, hurt, and sadness. Engaging in healthy emotional release activities such as writing in a journal, talking to a trusted friend or therapist, or engaging in creative outlets can be instrumental in letting go of negative emotions.

4. **Self-Reflection and Responsibility:** Part of cultivating forgiveness involves reflecting upon one's role in the situation. This self-reflection allows you to take responsibility for your actions and reactions. Identifying any personal contributions to the conflict can be humbling and aid the forgiveness process.

5. **Gratitude and Positive Focus:** Cultivating forgiveness requires shifting focus toward positive aspects of life and fostering gratitude. By consciously acknowledging and appreciating the blessings and positive experiences, you can recalibrate your mindset and create a fertile ground for forgiveness.

6. **Mindfulness and Meditation:** Practicing mindfulness and meditation can enhance self-awareness, promote emotional regulation, and improve overall well-being. By bringing attention to the present moment and observing thoughts and emotions non-judgmentally, you can gain clarity and find greater ease in forgiving.

7. **Seeking Support:** Forgiveness can be a challenging and deeply personal journey. Seeking support from friends, family, or professionals such as therapists or counselors can provide guidance, validation, and a safe environment to explore and navigate the complexities of forgiveness.

How to Cultivate Forgiveness

1. **Acceptance and Acknowledgment:** Accept the reality of the hurt or harm suffered. Acknowledge the pain experienced.

2. **Empathy and Perspective-Taking:** Put yourself in the other person's shoes. Strive to understand their motivations, struggles, and reasons for their actions.

3. **Emotional Release:** Acknowledge and express your feelings of anger, hurt, and sadness. Engage in healthy emotional release activities, such as journaling or talking to a trusted friend or therapist.

4. **Self-Reflection and Responsibility:** Reflect on your role in the situation. Take responsibility for your actions and reactions.

5. **Gratitude and Positive Focus:** Shift your focus towards positive aspects of life. Foster gratitude by acknowledging and appreciating blessings and positive experiences.

6. **Mindfulness and Meditation:** Practice mindfulness and meditation to enhance self-awareness. Observe thoughts and emotions non-judgmentally.

7. **Seeking Support:** Seek support from friends, family, or professionals. Find guidance, validation, and a safe environment to explore and navigate the complexities of forgiveness.

It is important to approach forgiveness with patience, dedication, and adherence to the established procedures. By following these strategies, you can embark on a transformative journey toward healing, growth, and overall well-being.

Forgiveness In Action

1. **Letting Go of Anger:** Mary experienced a betrayal by her best friend, which left her feeling angry and hurt. She decides to practice forgiveness by accepting her emotions and acknowledging the pain caused. Through therapy, she learns to express her anger in healthy ways and gradually lets go of the resentment she holds towards her friend. This emotional release allows her to rebuild their friendship and find peace within herself.

2. **Developing Empathy:** Fred's coworker constantly criticizes and undermines him, causing tension and animosity in their relationship. Instead of holding onto anger, Fred attempts to understand his coworker's motivations and struggles. By imagining what it might be like to be in his coworker's position, Fred develops empathy and realizes that the criticism stems from his coworker's insecurities. This understanding enables Fred to let go of resentment and foster a more positive work environment.

3. **Taking Responsibility**: After a heated argument with his partner, James reflects on his own words and actions during the conflict. He recognizes that he contributed to the disagreement by reacting defensively. By taking responsibility for his role in the situation, James acknowledges his flaws and apologizes to his partner. This act of self-reflection aids in repairing their relationship and promotes forgiveness between them.

4. **Shifting Focus:** Emma experienced a traumatic event that left her feeling angry and bitter about life. To cultivate forgiveness, she starts practicing gratitude by keeping a gratitude journal and consciously focusing on the positive aspects of her life. By redirecting her attention towards the blessings and joys, Emma finds a renewed sense of appreciation and begins to let go of the negativity that consumed her.

5. **Mindfulness Practice:** John's father abandoned him as a child, leaving him with deep emotional scars. To heal and forgive, John incorporates mindfulness and meditation into his daily routine.

Through mindfulness exercises, he learns to observe his thoughts and emotions without judgment, allowing him to gain clarity and distance himself from his past wounds. This newfound self-awareness helps John gradually let go of the anger and resentment towards his absent father.

6. **Seeking Support:** Maria went through a traumatic experience that affected her ability to trust others. Recognizing the need for guidance, Maria seeks support from a therapist who specializes in trauma and forgiveness. With the therapist's help, Maria embarks on a journey of inner healing, exploring her emotions and gradually working towards forgiveness. The therapist provides a safe space for Maria to express her feelings and offers valuable insights and strategies throughout the process.

7. By embracing forgiveness and utilizing these strategies, you can experience healing, personal growth, and a renewed sense of well-being.

The Power of Forgiveness in Healing Relationships

Susan and Emily had been best friends for over a decade, supporting each other through thick and thin. However, a misunderstanding led to a heated argument that tore their friendship apart. Susan felt betrayed, hurt, and angry, while Emily was remorseful but struggled to articulate her emotions. Both realized that forgiveness was necessary to heal their fractured relationship.

Actions and Initiatives Implemented

1. **Acceptance and Acknowledgment**: Susan and Emily acknowledged the pain they caused each other. They reflected on the specific incident, accepting the reality of the hurt experienced.

2. **Empathy and Perspective-Taking:** Susan and Emily practiced empathy and perspective-taking. They tried to understand each other's motivations, struggles, and reasons for their actions, allowing compassion and understanding to emerge.

3. **Emotional Release:** Susan and Emily engaged in healthy emotional release activities. Susan found solace in journaling her emotions and exploring her feelings with a trusted friend, while Emily sought therapy to work through her suppressed emotions.

4. **Self-Reflection and Responsibility:** Susan and Emily explored their roles in the conflict. They took responsibility for their actions, acknowledging their contributions to the deterioration of their friendship.

5. **Gratitude and Positive Focus:** Susan and Emily consciously shifted their focus towards gratitude and positive aspects of their lives. They expressed gratitude for the good times they shared and looked for opportunities to create new positive experiences together.

6. **Mindfulness and Meditation:** Susan and Emily practiced mindfulness and meditation to improve self-awareness judgmentally, they gained clarity and discovered inner peace.

7. **Seeking Support:** Susan and Emily recognized the need for external support. They sought help from a therapist who guided them through the forgiveness process, providing a safe environment to express their emotions and resolve conflicts.

Sarah And Emily Experienced Positive Outcomes

1. **Restoration of Friendship:** Susan and Emily successfully rebuilt their friendship. They reconnected on a deeper level, re-establishing trust, and a sense of security.

2. **Improved Well-being:** Susan and Emily reported improved mental and emotional well-being. They experienced reduced anger, resentment, and sadness, replaced by inner peace, joy, and contentment.

3. **Enhanced Communication:** Susan and Emily developed better communication skills, enabling them to express themselves honestly, listen actively, and navigate conflicts effectively.

Susan And Emily Encountered Challenges Throughout Their Forgiveness Journey

1. **Initial Resistance:** Initially, they resisted the idea of forgiveness. They struggled with skepticism, fear of vulnerability, and uncertainty about the outcome.

2. **Relapse and Triggers:** There were moments when old wounds resurfaced, leading to relapses in forgiveness. Triggers from past conflicts tested their commitment and required renewed efforts.

3. **Patience and Persistence:** Forgiveness is a gradual process that requires patience and persistence. Susan and Emily had to remind themselves of the long-term benefits, even when progress seemed slow or stagnant.

They Learned Valuable Lessons throughout Their Forgiveness Journey

1. **Forgiveness Takes Time:** They realized that forgiveness is not an overnight process. It requires consistent effort, self-reflection, and a willingness to let go of negative emotions.
2. **Empathy Promotes Healing:** Developing empathy and understanding the other person's perspective is crucial for healing fractured relationships. It allows space for compassion, forgiveness, and growth.
3. **External Support is Valuable:** Seeking support from trusted individuals or professionals is essential. Therapy played a vital role in their forgiveness process, providing guidance, validation, and a safe environment.

Overall Assessment Impact on Forgiveness

Susan and Emily's case study demonstrates the transformative power of forgiveness. By following a structured approach and incorporating forgiveness strategies, they were able to heal their relationship, improve their well-being, and develop a deeper understanding of themselves and each other. The measurable outcomes achieved highlight the profound impact forgiveness can have on mental, emotional, physical, and spiritual health.

It reaffirms the importance of forgiveness as a key component of overall well-being, underscoring its role in fostering healing, growth, and connection. Now that we have explored the inspiring case study of Susan and Emily and witnessed the transformative power of forgiveness in their relationship, let us delve into a comprehensive list of mistakes to avoid when embarking on a forgiveness journey.

Typical Mistakes And How To Avoid Them

1. **Holding onto anger, resentment, or bitterness:** Many people struggle to let go of negative emotions, which can have a detrimental impact on their mental and emotional well-being. To avoid this mistake, you need to acknowledge and accept their feelings and actively work towards forgiving the offender.

2. **Lack of empathy and perspective-taking:** Without understanding the other person's motivations and struggles, it is difficult to cultivate forgiveness. Taking the time to empathize with the offender's perspective can aid in the forgiveness process.

3. **Suppressing emotions:** Forgiveness does not mean denying or suppressing one's emotions. It is important to engage in healthy emotional release activities, such as writing, talking to a trusted friend or therapist, or engaging in creative outlets, to let go of negative emotions.

4. **Failure to self-reflect and take responsibility:** It is crucial to reflect on one's role in the situation and take responsibility for one's actions and reactions. By identifying personal contributions to the conflict, individuals can humbly navigate the forgiveness process.

5. **Neglecting gratitude and positive focus:** Shifting focus towards positive aspects of life and practicing gratitude is essential in cultivating forgiveness. By consciously acknowledging and appreciating blessings and positive experiences, you create a fertile ground for forgiveness.

6. **Lack of mindfulness and meditation:** Practicing mindfulness and meditation enhances self-awareness, emotional regulation, and overall well-being. By bringing attention to the present moment and observing thoughts and emotions non-judgmentally, you can find greater ease in forgiving.

7. **Not seeking support:** Forgiveness can be a challenging journey, and it is important to seek support from friends, family, or professionals like therapists and counselors. Their guidance and validation can provide a safe space to explore and navigate the complexities of forgiveness.

#1 Piece Of Advice

Let go of grudges, release the pain, and embrace forgiveness for inner healing and peace.

Summary

- Forgiveness has a profound impact on our mental, emotional, physical, and spiritual well-being, leading to greater health and happiness.

- Acceptance and acknowledgment of the pain experienced is the first step towards forgiveness, allowing individuals to gradually work towards forgiving the offender.

- Developing empathy by understanding the motivations and struggles of others can facilitate the forgiveness process.

- Engaging in healthy emotional release activities, such as writing in a journal or talking to a trusted friend, can help let go of negative emotions.

- Shifting focus towards gratitude and positive aspects of life creates a fertile ground for forgiveness and overall well-being.

Quiz

1. What is the primary role of forgiveness in our lives?

A. To free us from guilt

B. To enhance our mental, emotional, physical, and spiritual wellbeing

C. To restore relationships

D. To provide us with a sense of relief

2. What is the first step in the process of forgiveness?

A. Empathy and perspective-taking

B. Acceptance and acknowledgment

C. Gratitude and positive focus

D. Self-reflection and responsibility

3. What is the purpose of engaging in emotional release activities?

A. To become more mindful and present

B. To cultivate empathy for the other person

C. To recognize and appreciate blessings

D. To let go of negative emotions

4. What is the role of self-reflection in forgiveness?

A. To identify personal contributions to the conflict

B. To develop empathy for the offender

C. To shift focus towards positive aspects of life

D. To engage in healthy emotional release activities

5. What is the importance of seeking support during the forgiveness process?

A. To provide guidance, validation, and a safe environment

B. To cultivate gratitude and positive focus

C. To engage in mindfulness and *meditation*

D. To free oneself from guilt

Answer Key

1. B
2. B
3. D
4. A
5. A

As we have explored the profound impact of forgiveness on our overall well-being in the previous chapter. It is now time to dive into another powerful practice that can further enhance our mental, emotional, and spiritual health.

In the next chapter, we will discuss specific recommendations for incorporating mindfulness or meditation practices into our daily routines. Offering practical guidance on how to nurture inner peace and cultivate a deeper sense of fulfillment.

So, dear reader, if you are eager to discover life-changing techniques that will continue to enrich your well-being.

I encourage you to keep reading and unlock the transformative potential of mindfulness and meditation.

CHAPTER NINE

Journey Within: *The Transformative Power of Mindfulness and Meditation*

"In the stillness of meditation, we find the answers that cannot be heard in the noise of the outside world."

Incorporating mindfulness and meditation practices into one's routine can significantly enhance mental, emotional, and spiritual well-being. To maximize the benefits, it is crucial to approach these practices with intention, consistency, and a prop understanding of their principles.

Here Are Some Specific Recommendations

1. **Start small and gradually build up:** It is essential to approach mindfulness and meditation practices with realistic expectations. Begin by dedicating just a few minutes each day to these practices and gradually increase the duration over time. This gradual progression allows for a sustainable integration into your routine without overwhelming yourself.

2. **Find a quiet and comfortable space:** Creating a suitable environment for mindfulness and meditation is crucial. Choose a quiet and peaceful place where you can sit comfortably, free from distractions. This dedicated space will help you cultivate a sense of sacredness and tranquility during your practice.

3. **Set a regular schedule:** Consistency is key in developing a mindfulness and meditation routine. Set a specific time each day for your practice, whether it is in the morning, evening, or any other time that suits you best. By establishing a regular schedule, you are more likely to make mindfulness and meditation a habitual part of your daily routine.

4. **Begin with mindful breathing:** Mindful breathing is an excellent starting point for beginners. Sit in a comfortable position, close your eyes, and focus your attention on your breath. Observe the sensation of the breath entering and leaving your body, without trying to control it. Whenever your

mind wanders, gently bring your attention back to the breath. This practice cultivates present-moment awareness and serves as a foundation for other mindfulness techniques.

5. **Explore guided meditations or mindfulness apps**: Guided meditations can be particularly helpful for beginners or those who find it challenging to maintain focus. There are various apps and online resources available that offer guided meditations tailored to specific goals and preferences. These tools provide structured guidance, helping individuals deepen their practice and stay on track.

6. **Gradually expand your practice:** As you become more comfortable with basic mindfulness techniques, consider exploring different meditation styles or techniques that align with your goals and interests. Exploring a variety of practices allows for a more comprehensive cultivation of mental, emotional, and spiritual well-being.

7. **Seek guidance from a qualified person:** While self-guided practice can be beneficial, receiving guidance from a qualified person can greatly enhance your understanding and refinement of mindfulness and meditation practices. Look for experienced teachers or consider joining a meditation group or retreat to deepen your practice and gain valuable insights from others.

Remember, incorporating mindfulness and meditation into your routine requires commitment, patience, and consistency. It is through regular practice that the transformative power of these practices unfolds.

Be open to the process, have faith in the God of the Universe, and allow yourself to embark on a journey of self-discovery and growth.

Now that you have gained a deeper understanding of the principles and recommendations for incorporating mindfulness and meditation practices into your routine. It's time to put them into action. To help you stay on track and maximize the benefits, I have created a checklist that you can use as a guide.

- Start small and gradually build up your practice time.
- Find a quiet and comfortable space for your practice.
- Set a regular schedule for your mindfulness and meditation practice.
- Begin with mindful breathing as a simple yet effective technique.
- Explore guided meditations or mindfulness apps to help maintain focus.
- Gradually expand your practice by exploring different meditation styles or techniques.
- Seek guidance from a qualified meditation teacher to enhance your understanding and refinement.

- Be committed, patient, and consistent in your practice.
- Have faith in the God of the Universe.
- Embrace the journey of self-discovery and growth as you integrate these practices into your routine.

Now that we have gone through this checklist, let's look at some examples that illustrate how these practices can be incorporated into your daily routine.

- **Belle** wanted to start incorporating mindfulness and meditation into her daily routine. She began by dedicating five minutes each morning to sitting in a quiet corner of her living room and focusing on her breathing. Over the course of a few weeks, she gradually increased her practice to ten minutes, then fifteen, until she reached her goal of twenty minutes a day.

- **Justin** struggled to find a quiet space in his busy apartment for his mindfulness practice. He decided to convert a spare bedroom into a meditation room. He painted the walls a soothing color, placed a comfortable cushion on the floor, and added a small fountain to create a peaceful ambiance. This dedicated space helped Justin feel a sense of tranquility and sacredness during his practice.

- **Mavis** found it challenging to stick to a consistent meditation schedule due to her unpredictable work hours. She realized that she always had a few minutes to spare during her lunch break. So, she set aside ten minutes every day to meditate in the office breakroom. By creating a regular schedule that fits into her daily routine, Mary was able to make mindfulness and meditation a habitual part of her day.

- **Michael** was new to mindfulness and meditation, so he decided to start with mindful breathing. Every day, he dedicated five minutes to sitting on his porch and focusing on his breath. Whenever his mind wandered, he gently brought his attention back to the sensation of his breath. Over time, he noticed an increased sense of calm and clarity, which motivated him to continue exploring other mindfulness techniques.

- **Emily** found it difficult to maintain focus during meditation without any guidance. She decided to try a guided meditation app that provided step-by-step instructions. She found a guided meditation specifically designed for stress reduction and listened to it every evening before bed. The soothing voice and structured guidance helped Emily deepen her practice and stay on track.

- **Tim** had been practicing basic mindfulness techniques for a while and wanted to expand his practice. He decided to explore biblical meditation to cultivate compassion towards himself and others. He found that this practice helped him develop a greater sense of empathy and connectedness with the world around him. Tim realized that there were various meditation styles and techniques available, and he was excited to continue exploring and expanding his practice.
- **Lisa** had been practicing meditation for a few months but felt like she needed additional guidance and support. She decided to seek guidance from a qualified meditation teacher and enrolled in a mindfulness course. Through this course, she received personalized instruction, learned new techniques, and had the opportunity to ask questions and receive feedback. Being part of a supportive community also enriched Lisa's experience and helped her deepen her practice.

We have explored a range of examples showcasing different approaches to incorporating mindfulness and meditation into daily life. Let's look at a case study that highlights how mindfulness and meditation can be implemented in a corporate setting.

The objective is to enhance the mental, emotional, and spiritual well-being of employees, leading to improved productivity and overall job satisfaction.

Zab Corporation, a leading technology company, recognized the need to address employee stress and burnout. It was found that many employees were struggling to balance work and personal life, resulting in decreased productivity and job satisfaction.

Action Taken

1. **Start small and gradually build up:** The company introduced a 5-minute mindfulness practice in the morning as a starting point. Employees were encouraged to dedicate just a few minutes each day to mindfulness and meditation.
2. **Find a quiet and comfortable space:** Designated meditation rooms were created within the office premises. These rooms were soundproof and equipped with comfortable seating, allowing employees to sit comfortably and free from distractions.

3. **Set a regular schedule:** To ensure consistency, the company encouraged employees to set aside a specific time each day for mindfulness practice. Morning and afternoon sessions were offered to accommodate individual preferences.

4. **Begin with mindful breathing:** The mindfulness practice started with a focus on mindful breathing. Employees were guided to sit comfortably, close their eyes, and focus on their breath. This practice cultivated present-moment awareness and served as a foundation for other mindfulness techniques.

5. **Explore guided meditations or mindfulness apps:** To provide structured guidance, the company partnered with a mindfulness app that offered a variety of guided meditations. Employees were encouraged to explore different meditations tailored to their goals and interests.

Challenges Faced

1. **Gradually expand the practice:** As employees became more comfortable with basic mindfulness techniques, they were encouraged to explore different meditation styles and techniques.

2. **Seek guidance from a qualified teacher:** The company invited experienced meditation teachers to conduct workshops and retreats. Employees had the opportunity to deepen their practice and gain valuable insights from these teachers.

Measurable Outcomes

1. **Decreased stress levels:** Regular mindfulness and meditation practice resulted in reduced stress levels among employees. This was measured through pre and post-intervention surveys.

2. **Increased job satisfaction:** Employees reported higher job satisfaction and a sense of well-being after implementing mindfulness and meditation practices. This was measured through employee satisfaction surveys.

3. **Improved productivity:** The company observed an increase in productivity and focus among employees. Task completion rates and success metrics improved significantly.

4. **Resistance to change:** Some employees were skeptical about the effectiveness of mindfulness and meditation practices and initially resisted participating in the program.

5. **Sustaining commitment:** It was challenging for some employees to maintain consistency in their practice due to work-related demands and time constraints.

Lessons Learned

Patience and gradual progression are key in implementing mindfulness and meditation practices. Providing a conducive environment with designated spaces for practice is essential for cultivating a sense of sacredness and tranquility. Offering a variety of meditation techniques and resources that cater to individual preferences and goals. Seeking guidance from qualified teachers or experts enhances understanding and refinement of mindfulness and meditation practices. Regular evaluation and feedback from employees help refine the program and address any concerns or challenges faced.

Overall Assessment

The implementation of mindfulness and meditation practices in the corporate office had a significant impact on the mental, emotional, and spiritual well-being of the employees. It resulted in reduced stress levels, increased job satisfaction, and improved productivity. The program cultivated a culture of mindfulness and self-care, contributing to a more positive and harmonious work environment.

Typical Mistakes And How To Avoid Them

Based on the material covered, some mistakes that most people make in incorporating mindfulness and meditation practices into their routine include:

1. **Setting unrealistic expectations:** Many people expect immediate results from mindfulness and meditation practices. It is important to start small and gradually build up to avoid feeling overwhelmed and discouraged.
2. **Not creating a suitable environment:** Having a quiet and comfortable space dedicated to mindfulness and meditation helps cultivate a sense of tranquility. It is crucial to choose a peaceful place free from distractions to enhance the practice.
3. **Lack of consistency:** Establishing a regular schedule is essential for making mindfulness and meditation a habitual part of the daily routine. Without consistent practice, it becomes challenging to experience the full benefits.

4. **Not starting with mindful breathing:** Mindful breathing is a fundamental technique for beginners, yet some may overlook or underestimate its importance. Starting with this practice helps cultivate present-moment awareness and serves as a foundation for other mindfulness techniques.

5. **Not exploring guided meditations or mindfulness apps:** Guided meditations can provide structured guidance and help individuals maintain focus. Many people may not take advantage of these resources, which can support and deepen their practice.

6. **Sticking to one technique only:** It is beneficial to explore different meditation styles and techniques that align with one's goals and interests. Trying various practices allows for a more comprehensive cultivation of well-being.

7. **Not seeking guidance from a qualified teacher:** While self-guided practice is beneficial, receiving guidance from a qualified meditation teacher can enhance understanding and refinement of mindfulness and meditation practices. Seeking guidance from experienced teachers or joining a meditation group or retreat can provide valuable insights and support.

To avoid these common mistakes and truly experience the transformative power of mindfulness and meditation. It is important to approach them with a sense of commitment, patience, consistency, and openness to the process.

My #1 Piece Of Advice

Practice mindfulness and meditation regularly to cultivate inner peace, clarity, and self-awareness, transforming your mental, emotional, physical, and spiritual well-being.

Summary:

- Start small and gradually build up: Approach mindfulness and meditation with realistic expectations, dedicating just a few minutes each day and gradually increasing the duration over time.

- Find a quiet and comfortable space: Create a peaceful environment where you can sit comfortably, free from distractions, to cultivate a sense of sacredness and tranquility during your practice.

- Set a regular schedule: Consistency is key, so set a specific time each day for your mindfulness and meditation practice. This will help make it a habitual part of your routine.

- Begin with mindful breathing: Start with focusing on your breath, observing the sensations without trying to control it. Gently bring your attention back whenever your mind wanders.

- Explore guided meditations or mindfulness apps: Use these tools to deepen your practice and stay on track, as they provide structured guidance tailored to your goals and preferences.

Quiz

Q1. What is the recommended approach to incorporating mindfulness and meditation into one's routine?

A. Dedicate just a few minutes each day and gradually increase over time
B. Set a specific time each day for your practice
C. Explore guided meditations or mindfulness apps
D. All of the above

Q2. What is an important factor to consider when creating a suitable environment for mindfulness and meditation?
A. A quiet and peaceful space
B. A comfortable position
C. Free from distractions
D. All of the above

Q3. What is an effective starting point for beginners?

A. Mindful breathing

B. Loving-kindness meditation

C. Body scan meditation

D. Mindfulness of emotions

Q4. What type of guidance can be beneficial for deepening mindfulness and meditation practice?

A. Self-guided practice

B. Experienced teachers

C. Meditation groups

D. All of the above

Q5. What is the key to unlocking the transformative power of mindfulness and meditation?

A. Commitment

B. Patience

C. Consistency

D. All of the above

Answer Key

Q1. D

Q2. D

Q3. A

Q4. D

Q5. D

Now that you understand the benefits of mindfulness and meditation practice.

Let's explore the common challenges faced by individuals who may not be in a mentally, emotionally, physically, and spiritually healthy state, and discover ways you can overcome these obstacles.

Keep reading to gain valuable insights and practical advice on how to navigate these challenges and find inner well-being.

CHAPTER TEN

Overcoming the Unseen Barriers: *Conquering the Challenges of Mental, Emotional, Physical, and Spiritual Well-being*

"True healing occurs when we address the root causes of our challenges, rather than merely treating the symptoms. By digging deep and exploring the interplay between our mental, emotional, physical, and spiritual spheres, we can unlock lasting transformation."

In my extensive experience working with mentally, emotionally, physically, and spiritually unwell humans, I have encountered several common challenges or obstacles that hinder their path toward achieving optimal well-being. These challenges, although diverse in nature, share a common thread that revolves around the interplay between one's mental, emotional, physical, and spiritual spheres. To overcome these obstacles, a comprehensive approach is necessary, addressing each aspect holistically and with careful attention to detail. You may face challenges related to your cognitive functioning, such as distorted thinking patterns, negative self-talk, and difficulty in regulating emotions.

To overcome these challenges, cognitive-behavioral therapy (CBT), a powerful evidence-based technique, can prove immensely beneficial. CBT helps you reframe your thoughts and beliefs, challenge irrational thinking, and develop healthier coping strategies. Alongside therapy, adopting mindfulness practices and engaging in activities that promote cognitive stimulation can enhance mental well-being. Emotionally you may frequently experience difficulties in managing your emotions, which can manifest as anxiety, depression, or unresolved trauma.

Overcoming these challenges can be achieved through various modalities, including psychotherapy and counseling. Engaging in talk therapy allows you to process your emotions, develop healthier emotional regulation skills, and cultivate resilience. In some cases, incorporating techniques like dialectical behavior therapy (DBT) or eye movement desensitization and reprocessing (EMDR) can expedite emotional healing and build emotional stability. Regarding physical well-being, if you face challenges in this domain you may struggle with chronic illness, lack of energy, unhealthy lifestyle habits, or a sedentary lifestyle.

To overcome these hurdles, a multi-faceted approach is essential. Building a strong foundation through regular exercise, proper nutrition, and adequate sleep forms the cornerstone of physical well-being. Additionally, you should seek medical guidance to manage and treat any underlying physical conditions.

Engaging in activities that bring joy, practicing self-care, and fostering a supportive social network can also contribute significantly to physical wellness. Spiritual well-being plays a vital role in overall mental well-being, and you may often feel disconnected, lacking purpose, or grappling with existential questions. To address these challenges, you can explore practices that nurture your spiritual side, such as meditation, mindfulness, or engaging in religious or philosophical pursuits.

Reflecting on personal values, and purpose, and setting meaningful goals can provide direction and contribute to a sense of fulfillment and spiritual connectedness. Mentally, emotionally, physically, and spiritually you may face a range of challenges that hinder your pursuit of well-being. By adopting a comprehensive and holistic approach, incorporating therapeutic interventions, lifestyle modifications, self-care practices, and seeking appropriate professional guidance. You can navigate these obstacles and embark on a journey toward reclaiming your mental, emotional, physical, and spiritual invincibility.

Remember, the path to well-being is unique for everyone, and it is crucial to follow established procedures while remaining focused on achieving desired results. Here is a practical checklist that can serve as a guide to overcoming these obstacles and achieving optimal well-being.

1. **Mental Well-being:** Seek cognitive-behavioral therapy (CBT) to reframe thoughts and beliefs, challenge irrational thinking, and develop healthier coping strategies. Practice mindfulness to enhance mental well-being. Engage in activities that promote cognitive stimulation, such as puzzles or learning new skills.
2. **Emotional Well-being:** Consider psychotherapy or counseling to process emotions, develop healthy emotional regulation skills, and cultivate resilience. Explore techniques like dialectical behavior therapy (DBT) or eye movement desensitization and reprocessing (EMDR) for emotional healing. Prioritize self-care and engage in activities that bring joy.

3. **Physical Well-being:** Build a strong foundation by engaging in regular exercise, proper nutrition, and adequate sleep. Seek medical guidance to manage and treat any underlying physical conditions. Foster a supportive social network to contribute to physical wellness.

4. **Spiritual Well-being:** Explore practices that nurture the spiritual side, such as meditation, mindfulness, or engagement in religious or philosophical pursuits. Reflect on personal values, and purpose, and set meaningful goals to provide direction and a sense of fulfillment. Connect with a community or support network that shares similar spiritual beliefs or interests.

5. **Comprehensive Approach:** Adopt a holistic approach that addresses mental, emotional, physical, and spiritual well-being concurrently. Seek appropriate professional guidance from therapists, counselors, or medical practitioners. Customize the approach to suit individual needs and goals while following established procedures. Remember, the path to well-being is unique for everyone, and it may require ongoing adjustments and adaptations. Regularly reevaluate and refine the action steps as needed to continue progressing toward optimal well-being.

Now that we have gone through the action steps checklist for achieving optimal well-being, let's look at some examples that illustrate how these steps can be put into practice.

- **Jon** is a mentally unwell individual who struggles with distorted thinking patterns and negative self-talk. He constantly doubts his abilities and believes he is a failure. Through cognitive-behavioral therapy (CBT), Jon learns to challenge his irrational thoughts and reframe them more positively and realistically. With regular therapy sessions and practicing mindfulness, Jon gradually develops healthier coping strategies and experiences improved mental well-being.

- **Angel** is emotionally unwell and has been carrying unresolved trauma from her childhood. She experiences intense anxiety and struggles to regulate her emotions. With the help of psychotherapy and counseling, Angel can process her emotions, release her trauma, and learn new emotional regulation skills. She also incorporates eye movement desensitization and reprocessing (EMDR) techniques, which facilitate healing and provide relief from her emotional distress.

- **Michael** is physically unwell and has been diagnosed with a chronic illness that causes constant fatigue and pain. He also leads a sedentary lifestyle and has poor eating habits. To overcome these challenges, Michael starts by seeking medical guidance to manage his condition. He then incorporates regular exercise into his routine, follows a balanced diet, and ensures he gets enough rest. Through these lifestyle modifications, Michael's physical well-being gradually improves, and he experiences increased energy and a reduction in symptoms.

- **Rachel** is spiritually unwell and feels disconnected and purposeless. She embarks on a journey of self-discovery and starts practicing meditation and mindfulness. She also explores different religious and philosophical teachings to find meaning and purpose in her life. As Rachel reflects on her personal values and sets meaningful goals, she gradually reconnects with her spiritual side and experiences a sense of fulfillment and connectedness.

- **Alex** is a mentally, emotionally, physically, and spiritually unwell individual. He struggles with depression, has unresolved trauma, lacks energy due to a sedentary lifestyle, and feels disconnected from his spiritual side. To address these challenges comprehensively, Alex starts by seeking therapy to address his mental and emotional well-being. He incorporates regular exercise and healthy eating habits to improve his physical well-being. He also explores mindfulness and engages in practices that nurture his spiritual side. Through this holistic approach, Alex can overcome his obstacles and achieve a balanced state of well-being.

Overcoming Obstacles to Achieve Mental Well-Being

Tarah is a 35-year-old woman who has been experiencing symptoms of anxiety and depression for several years. She often feels overwhelmed, struggles with negative self-talk, and finds it challenging to regulate her emotions. Tarah also leads a sedentary lifestyle and has been diagnosed with a chronic illness, which further impacts her overall well-being.

Challenges Faced

Tarah's mental well-being is affected by distorted thinking patterns, negative self-talk, and difficulty in regulating emotions. Additionally, her physical well-being is compromised due to a sedentary lifestyle and chronic illness.

1. **Cognitive-Behavioral Therapy (CBT):** Tarah engages in CBT sessions with a licensed therapist to reframe her thoughts, challenge irrational thinking, and develop healthier coping strategies.
2. **Mindfulness Practices:** Tarah incorporates mindfulness into her daily routine through meditation and engaging in activities that promote cognitive stimulation, such as puzzles and reading.

3. **Psychotherapy and Counseling:** Tarah attends talk therapy sessions to process her emotions, develop healthier emotional regulation skills, and cultivate resilience.
4. **Dialectical Behavior Therapy (DBT):** Tarah incorporates DBT techniques, such as mindfulness exercises and emotional regulation strategies, to expedite emotional healing and build emotional stability.
5. **Physical Activity and Nutrition:** Tarah adopts a multi-faceted approach to physical well-being. She starts exercising regularly, incorporating both cardio and strength training exercises. She consults a nutritionist to improve her diet, focusing on whole foods and adequate hydration.
6. **Medical Guidance:** Tarah seeks medical guidance to manage her chronic illness and receive appropriate treatment, ensuring that her physical health is addressed alongside her mental well-being.
7. **Self-Care Practices:** Tarah engages in activities that bring her joy, such as painting and spending time in nature. She prioritizes self-care, ensuring she takes time for herself and engages in activities that promote relaxation and rejuvenation.
8. **Spiritual Nurturing:** Tarah explores practices that nurture her spiritual side, including meditation. She also reflects on her personal values, and purpose, and sets meaningful goals to provide direction and cultivate a sense of fulfillment.

Measurable Outcomes

1. **Cognitive improvements:** Tarah experiences a reduction in distorted thinking patterns and negative self-talk. She develops healthier coping strategies and displays an improved ability to regulate her emotions.
2. **Emotional well-being:** Tarah's anxiety and depressive symptoms decreased, and she reports feeling more resilient and emotionally stable.
3. **Physical improvements:** Tarah's sedentary lifestyle is replaced with regular exercise, resulting in increased energy levels, and improved overall physical health. She successfully manages her chronic illness through medical guidance.
4. **Spiritual connectedness:** Tarah feels more connected and fulfilled, as she explores and nurtures her spiritual side through meditation and reflecting on personal values and purpose.

Challenges Faced

Tarah initially struggles with incorporating lifestyle changes, such as regular exercise and nutrition improvements. Additionally, addressing her chronic illness requires ongoing medical management, which poses its own set of challenges.

Lessons Learned

A comprehensive and holistic approach is essential, addressing mental, emotional, physical, and spiritual well-being simultaneously. Professional guidance and therapy sessions provide valuable tools and support in overcoming obstacles to well-being.

Persistence is key when implementing lifestyle changes, as it may take time to form new habits and see measurable results.

Assessment of Impact

By adopting a comprehensive approach and implementing various therapies, lifestyle modifications, and self-care practices, Tarah successfully overcame the obstacles that hindered her mental well-being. She experiences improvements in cognitive functioning, emotional well-being, physical health, and spiritual connectedness.

Tarah's journey demonstrates the effectiveness of addressing multiple dimensions of well-being to overcome challenges and achieve optimal mental wellness. Now that we have explored Tarah's journey toward achieving optimal mental well-being, let's dive into a list of mistakes to avoid when pursuing a similar path.

Typical Mistakes And How To Avoid Them

One common mistake people make in achieving optimal well-being is neglecting the interplay between their mental, emotional, physical, and spiritual spheres. To avoid this, you should adopt a comprehensive and holistic approach, addressing each aspect carefully and attentively.

Another mistake is not seeking appropriate professional guidance. You should not hesitate to engage in therapies such as cognitive-behavioral therapy (CBT), psychotherapy, counseling, dialectical behavior therapy (DBT), or eye movement desensitization and reprocessing (EMDR) to address mental and emotional challenges effectively.

Furthermore, neglecting physical well-being is a mistake many people make. To overcome this, you should focus on building a strong foundation through regular exercise, proper nutrition, and adequate sleep. Seeking medical guidance for underlying physical conditions is also crucial.

Lastly, ignoring spiritual well-being can hinder overall mental well-being. To avoid this mistake, you should explore practices such as meditation, mindfulness, or engaging in religious or philosophical pursuits. Reflecting on personal values, and purpose, and setting meaningful goals can provide direction and contribute to a sense of fulfillment and spiritual connectedness.

Now that we have looked at some common mistakes to avoid in achieving optimal well-being, it's important to remember that taking a comprehensive and holistic approach is key. With that in mind, my number one piece of advice is to prioritize self-care and make it a non-negotiable part of your daily routine.

My #1 Piece Of Advice

Acceptance is the key to overcoming obstacles and achieving mental well-being.

Summary

- Overcoming challenges requires a comprehensive approach that addresses mental, emotional, physical, and spiritual well-being.

- Cognitive-behavioral therapy (CBT) can help reframe thoughts, challenge irrational thinking, and develop healthier coping strategies.

- Talk therapy and modalities like dialectical behavior therapy (DBT) and eye movement desensitization and reprocessing (EMDR) can expedite emotional healing and build resilience.

- Building a strong foundation through exercise, nutrition, sleep, and medical guidance can greatly improve physical well-being.

- Nurturing spirituality through practices like meditation, mindfulness, yoga, and reflection on values and goals can provide fulfillment and reconnect with a sense of purpose.

Quiz

1. What is the primary focus of this material?

A. Cognitive-behavioral therapy (CBT)

B. Dialectical behavior therapy (DBT)

C. Eye movement desensitization and reprocessing (EMDR)

D. A comprehensive approach to achieving optimal well-being

2. What type of therapy is used to help individuals reframe their thoughts and beliefs?

A. Dialectical behavior therapy (DBT)

B. Eye movement desensitization and reprocessing (EMDR)

C. Cognitive-behavioral therapy (CBT)

D. Psychotherapy and counseling

3. What is an essential foundation for physical well-being?

A. Adopting mindfulness practices

B. Engaging in talk therapy

C. Regular exercise, proper nutrition, and adequate sleep

D. Exploring spiritual practices

4. How can individuals address spiritual challenges?

A. Through medical guidance

B. By incorporating techniques like DBT or EMDR

C. Through reflection on personal values, purpose, and setting meaningful goals

D. Engaging in religious or philosophical pursuits

5. What is the key to navigating obstacles to mental, emotional, physical, and spiritual well-being?

A. A comprehensive and holistic approach

B. Adopting mindfulness practices

C. Engaging in talk therapy

D. Seeking medical guidance

Answer Key

1. D

2. C

3. C

4. C

5. A

We have explored the common challenges and obstacles faced by mentally, emotionally, physically, and spiritually unwell individuals.

It is now time to dig into real-life examples and stories of individuals who have triumphed over these hurdles and experienced transformative changes, ultimately leading them to achieve holistic well-being and a strong relationship with God.

So, keep reading to discover the inspiring principles that can guide us toward our own personal transformations and a deep connection with our spirituality.

CHAPTER ELEVEN

Tales of Transformation: *Stories of Holistic Well-being and God's Impactful Guidance*

"Be mindful of the impact of your actions, for they shape your destiny."

I am thrilled to share stories of individuals who have successfully transformed their lives and achieved holistic well-being along with a strong relationship with God through the principles I teach. These individuals have implemented the concepts and techniques I advocate, allowing them to experience profound personal growth and spiritual enlightenment. I will provide two distinct examples to illustrate the transformative power of these principles.

The first example is Sarah, a middle-aged woman struggling with chronic anxiety, depression, and a lack of purpose in her life. Sarah had been prescribed various medications and had sought therapy for years, yet she felt trapped in a cycle of negativity and dissatisfaction. Upon coming across my book, *"The Greatest Truth in the Universe"*, she decided to embark on a journey of self-discovery and inner healing. Sarah began by incorporating mindfulness practices into her daily routine, such as meditation and journaling.

Through these practices, she gained clarity and a deeper understanding of her thoughts and emotions. Sarah learned to identify and challenge negative patterns of thinking, gradually replacing them with positive and empowering beliefs. She immersed herself in my teachings on self-compassion and self-care. She prioritized her physical well-being by adopting a healthier diet, exercising regularly, and getting enough restorative sleep.

Sarah also embraced spiritual practices like prayer and reflection, nurturing her relationship with God and finding solace in her faith. Over time, Sarah began to experience a profound shift in her well-being. Her anxiety and depression diminished significantly, and she developed a renewed sense of purpose and fulfillment. Sarah's relationships improved as she became more self-aware and compassionate towards others. Most importantly, her connection with God deepened, providing her with strength, guidance, and a profound source of peace and love.

The second example is Michael, a young man who had lost his way, battling addiction and a sense of hopelessness. Michael had hit rock bottom and knew that a radical change was necessary to reclaim his life. When I met him, he felt a glimmer of hope for the first time in years.

Michael committed himself to the principles I teach, seeking the guidance and support he needed to break free from his destructive habits. He engaged in a comprehensive recovery program that incorporated psychological, physical, and spiritual healing. Through therapy and counseling, Michael confronted the underlying traumas and emotional wounds that fueled his addiction.

He learned coping strategies and developed a support system that encouraged his sobriety. Michael also adopted healthy habits such as regular exercise, proper nutrition, and practicing mindfulness techniques to manage stress and cravings. As Michael progressed on his journey, he discovered a deeper connection with God and spirituality. He attended religious services, engaged in prayer and meditation, and sought guidance from spiritual mentors. Through these practices, Michael found the strength and resilience necessary to maintain his sobriety and rebuild his life.

Today, both Sarah and Michael serve as inspiring examples of individuals who have transformed their lives and achieved holistic well-being while forging a strong relationship with God. Their stories exemplify the power of implementing the principles I teach, which, emphasize self-awareness, self-compassion, physical health, and spiritual growth. By embracing these principles and following established procedures, you, like Sarah and Michael, can successfully navigate your challenges and create a meaningful, purpose-driven life. Now that you've read about the transformative power of the principles I teach through the stories of Sarah and Michael. I am excited to introduce the checklist I have created.

This checklist serves as a helpful guide for individuals looking to implement these principles and achieve holistic well-being while cultivating a strong relationship with God.

1. **Incorporate mindfulness practices into your daily routine**, such as meditation and journaling, to gain clarity and a deeper understanding of your thoughts and emotions.

2. **Identify and challenge negative patterns of thinking,** gradually replacing them with positive and empowering beliefs.

3. **Prioritize physical well-being by adopting a healthier diet,** exercising regularly, and getting enough restorative sleep.

4. **Embrace self-compassion and self-care practices,** to nurture your overall well-being.

5. **Engage in spiritual practices,** like prayer and reflection to nurture your relationship with God and find solace in your faith.

6. **Seek guidance and support from professionals,** such as therapists or counselors, to address underlying traumas and emotional wounds.

7. **Develop coping strategies** and a support system that encourages your personal growth and recovery.

8. **Adopt healthy habits,** such as regular exercise, proper nutrition, and mindfulness techniques to manage stress and cravings.\

9. **Engage in religious services,** prayer, and meditation to deepen your connection with God and spirituality.

10. **Embrace the principles of self-awareness,** self-compassion, physical health, and spiritual growth to navigate personal challenges and create a meaningful, purpose-driven life.

These guidelines are based on the transformative experiences of Sarah and Michael, who have achieved holistic well-being and a strong relationship with God through the principles taught.

Now that we have gone through this comprehensive checklist, let's take a closer look at how these principles have been applied as an example in the lives of two new individuals, **Emily and John. Emily** was a young woman who struggled with low self-esteem and a constant feeling of inadequacy. She had difficulty forming meaningful relationships and often found herself stuck in negative patterns of thinking. One day, Emily came across my book, *"The Greatest Truth in the Universe"* which emphasized the importance of self-love and self-acceptance.

She decided to embark on a journey of self-discovery and personal growth. Emily began practicing affirmations and positive self-talk daily to replace the negative thoughts that had held her back. She also committed to learning more about her strengths and passions and pursued activities that brought her joy and fulfillment. Emily attended therapy and sought guidance from mentors who helped her navigate her insecurities and develop a stronger sense of self.

As time went on, Emily experienced a profound transformation. She began to see herself in a more positive light and recognize her worth. Her relationships improved, and she formed deeper connections with others.

Emily's newfound self-confidence and self-acceptance allowed her to pursue her dreams and live a more empowered, purposeful life.

John was a successful businessman who had achieved material wealth but felt a constant emptiness in his life. He longed for a deeper sense of meaning and purpose. After coming across my book, *"The Greatest Truth in the Universe"* which emphasized spiritual growth and connection with a higher power, John decided to explore his spirituality. John began by incorporating daily gratitude practices into his routine. He expressed his appreciation for the blessings in his life and started looking for opportunities to show kindness and compassion to others.

He also adopted a regular meditation practice, which allowed him to quiet his mind and connect with God. As John deepened his spiritual journey, he started to notice a shift in his overall well-being. He felt a sense of peace and contentment that he had never experienced before. John began to see the beauty in the world around him and felt a deeper connection to nature and his fellow human beings. He also found that his decision-making became more aligned with his values, and he prioritized making a positive impact on the lives of others.

Transformative Power

These examples demonstrate the transformative power of implementing the principles discussed earlier. Whether it's overcoming anxiety and depression, battling addiction, struggling with low self-esteem, or searching for meaning and purpose. You can achieve profound personal growth and spiritual enlightenment by embracing self-awareness, self-compassion, physical health, and spiritual growth.

Through these practices, like Emily and John, you can navigate your challenges, find fulfillment, and experience God.

Typical Mistakes And How To Avoid Them

1. **Neglecting self-awareness and self-reflection:** You may not prioritize taking the time to understand your thoughts, emotions, and negative patterns of thinking. By incorporating mindfulness practices like meditation and journaling, you can gain clarity and develop a deeper understanding of yourself.

2. **Overlooking the importance of physical well-being:** You may neglect your physical health, which can have a significant impact on your overall well-being. Prioritizing a healthy diet, regular exercise and adequate sleep can contribute to your holistic well-being and personal growth.

3. **Disregarding the role of spiritual practices:** You may not recognize the potential benefits of nurturing your spirituality and relationship with God. Engaging in practices like prayer, reflection, and seeking guidance from spiritual mentors can provide strength, guidance, and peace.

My #1 Piece Of Advice

Learn to forgive yourself, embrace growth, and heal from your mistakes.

Summary

- Discover the transformative power of implementing these principles and techniques to experience profound personal growth and spiritual enlightenment.

- Prioritize self-care and self-compassion to improve physical and mental well-being, as exemplified by Sarah's journey to overcome chronic anxiety and depression.

- Embrace mindfulness practices, such as meditation and journaling, to gain clarity, challenge negative thought patterns, and replace them with positive and empowering beliefs.

- Nurture your relationship with God and find solace in your faith, following Sarah's example of incorporating spiritual practices like prayer and reflection.

- Break free from destructive habits and reclaim your life by engaging in a comprehensive recovery program that incorporates psychological, physical, and spiritual healing.

Quiz

1. What are the two examples used in the material?

A. Sarah and Michael

B. Jane and John

C. Alex and Ryan

D. Sam and Amy

2. What are some of the practices Sarah adopted to prioritize her physical well-being?

A. Eating junk food and skipping meals

B. Developing a healthy diet, exercising regularly, and getting restorative sleep

C. Doing yoga and getting acupuncture

D. Taking medication and going to therapy

3. What did Michael commit himself to to break free from his destructive habits?

A. A comprehensive recovery program

B. A daily meditation practice

C. A diet of only organic food

D. A strict exercise regime

4. What did Sarah learn to do to gain clarity and a deeper understanding of her thoughts and emotions?

A. Journaling

B. Writing down her dreams

C. Painting

D. Going on walks

5. What did Sarah and Michael have in common?

A. They both experienced a profound shift in their well-being

B. They both lived in the same city

C. They both sought therapy

D. They both had successful careers

Answer Key

1. A. Sarah and Michael

2. B. Developing a healthy diet, exercising regularly, and getting restorative sleep

3. A. A comprehensive recovery program

4. A. Journaling

5. A. They both experienced a profound shift in their well-being

Now we have seen inspiring examples of individuals who have embraced the principles and experienced transformative growth in their lives.

The next chapter delves into the practical strategies for maintaining consistency and motivation in the pursuit of holistic well-being and a meaningful relationship with God, even during challenging times or periods of spiritual dryness.

Keep reading to discover invaluable insights and encouragement on staying on track with your journey.

CHAPTER TWELVE

The Unwavering Journey: *Staying Motivated in the Pursuit of Well-Being and Faith, Regardless of Circumstances*

"It does not matter how slowly you go as long as you do not stop." – Confucius
"The only person you should try to be better than is the person you were yesterday." - Unknown

In the pursuit of achieving holistic well-being, you need to exhibit consistency. Maintain motivation throughout your journey towards becoming mentally, emotionally, physically, and spiritually well, as you pursue your personal relationship with God. This is particularly crucial during times of difficulty or spiritual dryness when the challenges can easily hinder progress. To address this, it is imperative to adopt a multifaceted approach that encompasses various strategies and practices. Establishing and adhering to a structured routine can provide a strong foundation for consistency. Creating a daily schedule that includes specific time slots dedicated to mental, emotional, physical, and spiritual well-being can help ensure that each aspect is given due attention.

This routine should incorporate activities such as meditation, prayer, exercise, self-reflection, and engaging in activities that bring joy and fulfillment. By assigning specific time for these practices, you can develop good habits and reinforce your commitment to your overall well-being. It is crucial to set realistic goals and track progress. Clearly defining objectives related to mental, emotional, physical, and spiritual growth can provide individuals with a sense of purpose and direction.

These goals should be Specific, Measurable, Achievable, Relevant, and Time-Bound. (**SMART** goals)

Regularly reviewing and evaluating progress toward these goals can help you celebrate small victories and maintain a positive mindset so you can further fuel your motivation. Incorporating community support is invaluable in sustaining motivation and consistency. Connecting with like-minded individuals who share similar aspirations can provide encouragement, inspiration, and accountability.

This can be achieved through joining support groups or engaging in online communities. You can also seek out mentors or spiritual advisors, attend religious services or gatherings, or participate in group activities centered around wellness. Engaging in meaningful conversations, sharing experiences, and seeking guidance from others, can help you navigate through challenging times and overcome spiritual dryness. During difficult periods, it is important to recognize that setbacks and obstacles are inevitable. However, maintaining motivation and consistency requires resilience and perseverance. Adopting a growth mindset and reframing difficulties as opportunities for learning can help you regain your footing.

Seeking knowledge through reading, studying scripture, attending workshops, and engaging in activities that stress personal growth can provide you with new perspectives and insights to navigate through these challenges. Furthermore, practicing self-compassion is crucial during times of difficulty. It is important to recognize that setbacks are part of the journey and to avoid self-criticism or negative self-talk. Cultivating self-care practices and engaging in activities that promote self-compassion, can be instrumental in maintaining motivation and emotional well-being.

Maintaining consistency and motivation in the journey towards becoming mentally, emotionally, physically, and spiritually well humans with a relationship with God requires a multifaceted approach. Establishing a structured routine, setting realistic goals, tracking progress, seeking community support, reframing challenges as opportunities, and practicing self-compassion are essential strategies. By adhering to these practices, you can navigate through times of difficulty or spiritual dryness and continue your path toward holistic well-being with strengthened motivation and unwavering dedication. Now that you have read about the multifaceted approach to maintaining consistency and motivation in your journey toward holistic well-being, it's time to put these strategies into action.

I have created a checklist that outlines the key steps and practices discussed in this article, ensuring that you have a tangible tool to help you stay on track.

- Establish and adhere to a structured routine that includes specific time slots for mental, emotional, physical, and spiritual well-being activities.
- Create **SMART** goals that are specific, measurable, attainable, relevant, and time-bound.
- Regularly review and evaluate progress toward goals.
- Celebrate small victories along the way.

- Seek community support through support groups, online communities, mentors, or spiritual advisors.
- Engage in meaningful conversations and share experiences with like-minded individuals.
- Recognize setbacks and obstacles as part of the journey and adopt a growth mindset.
- Seek knowledge through reading, studying scripture, and attending workshops.
- Practice self-compassion and avoid self-criticism or negative self-talk.
- Cultivate self-care practices such as journaling, practicing gratitude, and seeking professional help when needed.

Stay motivated and dedicated to holistic well-being with unwavering commitment.

Let's take a closer look at some examples that demonstrate how implementing these practices can benefit your holistic well-being.

- **John** wants to improve his mental well-being, so he establishes a structured routine that includes 30 minutes of meditation every morning before work. By consistently dedicating this time to meditation, John strengthens his mental well-being and maintains his motivation to continue this practice.
- **Sarah** sets a realistic goal of running a 5K race within six months to improve her physical well-being. She tracks her progress by keeping a running log and gradually increasing her mileage each week. As she sees her progress, Sarah stays motivated and continues to work towards her goal.
- **Maria** feels spiritually dry and lacks motivation in her relationship with God. She decided to join a Bible study group at her church to seek community support and engage in meaningful conversations about faith. By sharing her struggles and seeking guidance from others, Maria finds the encouragement she needs to overcome her spiritual dryness and stay motivated in her spiritual journey.
- **Tom** faces a setback in his emotional well-being after losing his job. Instead of letting this setback discourage him, he adopts a growth mindset and sees it as an opportunity for personal growth. Tom seeks knowledge by attending workshops on career development and networking, which helps him regain his motivation and find new job opportunities.
- **Lisa** experiences a period of difficulty in her mental well-being and feels overwhelmed with negative self-talk. She practices self-compassion by journaling about her emotions, practicing

gratitude for the positive aspects of her life, and seeking therapy to address her mental health needs. Through these self-care practices, Lisa maintains her motivation and takes proactive steps toward improving her mental well-being.

Now that we have seen several examples of individuals improving their well-being and maintaining their motivation, let's look into a case study that explores how a combination of strategies can contribute to overall well-being and motivation.

Background: John is a 35-year-old man who has been struggling with his overall well-being. He often feels mentally and emotionally drained, lacks physical energy, and has been experiencing a spiritual dryness.

Challenges Faced

John's biggest challenge is maintaining consistency and motivation in his journey towards holistic well-being. He finds it difficult to stay committed to self-improvement practices during difficult times, and his lack of routine and clear goals hinders his progress. Moreover, John feels isolated and lacks a support system to hold him accountable and inspire him.

Actions Taken

Recognizing the need for a multifaceted approach, John takes several specific actions to address his challenges. Firstly, he creates a structured routine by dedicating specific time slots each day to mental, emotional, physical, and spiritual activities. He starts his day with meditation and prayer, exercises in the afternoon, engages in self-reflection in the evening, and participates in activities that bring him joy before bed.

To ensure his progress is measurable, John sets SMART goals related to each aspect of his well-being. For example, he sets a goal to meditate for 10 minutes each day, exercise for 30 minutes three times a week, read self-help books to foster personal growth, and attend religious services regularly. John actively seeks community support by joining an online wellness group. He connects with like-minded individuals who are on a similar journey and participates in group activities centered around well-being.

He engages in meaningful conversations, shares his experiences, and seeks guidance from others. When facing setbacks or challenges, John adopts a growth mindset and reframes difficulties as opportunities for learning. He looks for workshops, attends religious seminars, and seeks knowledge to gain new perspectives and insights. He also practices self-compassion by journaling, practicing gratitude, and seeking professional help when needed.

Measurable Outcomes

As a result of his actions and initiatives, John experiences measurable outcomes. He observes that his mental clarity and emotional stability have improved significantly. He feels more energized and physically fit due to regular exercise. Spiritually, John finds solace in attending religious services and his relationship with God has deepened. He achieves most of his SMART goals, celebrating small victories along the way, which further fuels his motivation.

Challenges Faced and Lessons Learned

Throughout the journey, John faces challenges such as occasional lack of motivation and self-doubt. He realizes that setbacks are a part of the process and reframes them as learning opportunities. John learns the importance of seeking support and finding like-minded individuals who can provide encouragement and accountability. He understands the significance of self-compassion and the role it plays in maintaining motivation during difficult times.

Overall Assessment of Impact on Reaching the Wellness Paradigm

By adopting a multifaceted approach and implementing specific actions and initiatives, John has made significant progress toward the wellness paradigm. Structured routine, set goals, community support, reframing challenges, and practicing self-compassion have all played a crucial role in maintaining his consistency and motivation. John now feels more mentally, emotionally, physically, and spiritually well-rounded, and his strengthened relationship with God has brought him a sense of peace and fulfillment. He is on the right path toward achieving holistic well-being.

Now let's look at some of the mistakes to avoid maintaining consistency and motivation on the path to reach the Wellness Paradigm.

Typical Mistakes And How To Avoid Them

One mistake that most people make in the pursuit of holistic well-being is a lack of consistency and motivation. This can be avoided by establishing and adhering to a structured routine that includes specific time slots dedicated to mental, emotional, physical, and spiritual well-being. Setting realistic and measurable goals and time-bound can also help you stay motivated and track your progress. In addition, seeking community support and reframing challenges as opportunities for learning are crucial in maintaining motivation.

Practicing self-compassion and engaging in self-care practices can help you navigate through difficult periods and maintain emotional well-being.

My #1 Piece Of Advice

Self-compassion - prioritize nurturing yourself, accepting imperfections, and showing kindness towards yourself, which can lead to mental, emotional, physical, and spiritual well-being.

Summary

- Establish a structured routine that includes dedicated time for mental, emotional, physical, and spiritual well-being, allowing you to develop healthy habits and reinforce your commitment to holistic well-being.

- Set realistic goals and track your progress through measurable objectives, providing a sense of purpose and direction in your journey toward self-improvement.

- Seek community support from like-minded individuals who can inspire, encourage, and hold you accountable, helping you navigate through challenges and overcome spiritual dryness.

- Embrace setbacks and obstacles as learning opportunities, adopting a growth mindset that fuels resilience and perseverance in the face of difficulty.

- Practice self-compassion by avoiding self-criticism, engaging in self-care activities, and seeking professional help when needed, ensuring your emotional well-being, and maintaining motivation on your path towards holistic well-being.

QUIZ

1. What is the main purpose of establishing a structured routine in the journey towards holistic well-being?
    - A) To provide a sense of purpose and direction
    - B) To help ensure that each aspect of well-being is given due attention
    - C) To reinforce commitment to overall well-being
    - D) To provide a strong foundation for consistence

2. What is the acronym for goal setting to ensure they are specific, measurable, attainable, relevant, and time-bound (SMART)?

    - A) Specific, Measurable, Achievable, Relevant, and Time-limited
    - B) Specific, Measurable, Attainable, Relevant, and Time-bound
    - A) Strategic, Measurable, Attainable, Relevant, and Time-limited
    - B) Strategic, Measurable, Achievable, Relevant, and Time-bound

3. . What is the primary purpose of connecting with like-minded individuals
    - A) To provide encouragement and inspiration
    - B) To provide guidance and accountability
    - C) To provide support and direction
    - D) To provide motivation and consistency

4. What is a key mindset to adopt during times of difficulty or spiritual dryness?

   A) A fixed mindset

   B) A negative mindset

   C) A growth mindset

   D) A positive mindset

5. What is an example of an activity that could help individuals maintain motivation and emotional well-being?

   A) Reading

   B) Attending religious services

   C) Journaling

   D) Attending workshops

Answer Key

1. D

2. B

3. A

4. C

5. C

Our journey toward holistic well-being and a meaningful connection with God is an ongoing process. Together, we have explored powerful strategies and insights to help you maintain your progress, overcome obstacles, and nourish your spirituality.

Now, it's your turn to put the knowledge you have learned to the test.

It's time for you to transform that knowledge into wisdom.

And let that wisdom guide you through the land of understanding.

Where you will find the key that unlocks the door to the Universe.

Stay tuned, for there are still valuable nuggets of wisdom that lie ahead, awaiting your discovery!

Conclusion

Embracing Your Journey towards Wellness and Spiritual Awakening

Congratulations! You have reached the end of "The Wellness Paradigm: Mastering the Art of Mental, Emotional, Physical and Spiritual Awakening." I hope you feel a renewed sense of empowerment and clarity, armed with practical tools and examples to help you become the mentally, emotionally, physically, and spiritually well human you have always desired to be. Throughout this journey, you have embarked on a path of self-discovery, enabling you to recognize the areas in your life that require attention and nurturing.

You have gained valuable insights on how to foster mental resilience, cultivate emotional intelligence, optimize physical well-being, and nourish your soul. It is now time to put all that you have learned into practice, and I encourage you to take immediate action. Remember, true growth and transformation occur when knowledge is applied. You possess a wealth of practical advice, and tips, tailored to your unique needs. Now is the opportune moment to implement these strategies within your everyday life, infusing them with intentionality and steadfast determination. Embracing the wellness paradigm involves making conscious choices and taking deliberate steps toward your desired outcome.

Begin by setting achievable goals that align with your newfound understanding of what it means to be whole in mind, body, and spirit. These goals will vary for each individual, as we all have different areas that require attention. Be patient with yourself and embrace this process as a lifelong journey rather than a quick fix. In understanding your relationship with God, you have discovered a powerful source of strength, solace, and guidance. Nurture this connection by allowing yourself moments of reflection, prayer, and contemplation. Seek divine wisdom to steer you through challenges and to celebrate joys.

Remember, your relationship with God is personal and unique, and it will grow and evolve as you do. As you embark on this transformative chapter of your life, you may encounter obstacles and setbacks.

These are not signs of failure but rather growth opportunities. Embrace them with resilience and gratitude, knowing that each challenge is a chance to learn, adapt, and become stronger. Surround yourself with a support system of like-minded individuals who share your desire for wellness and spiritual awakening.

Engage in meaningful conversations, share your experiences, and uplift one another on this journey. Remember, you are not alone, and together, we can strive towards a brighter, more fulfilling future. Now, take a moment – right here, right now – to envision the ideal human you have always aspired to be. Imagine waking up each morning with a renewed sense of purpose and joy. Envision embracing mental clarity, emotional resilience, optimal physical health, and a deep spiritual connection.

This vision is not merely a dream; it is within your reach. So, my friend, don't delay. Begin today, right now. Empower yourself to live the life you have always desired, true transformation is not found in merely reading and understanding, but rather in taking action. May your journey toward wellness and spiritual awakening be marked by patience, growth, and the boundless love of God. Take the tools you have acquired, wield them with intention, and watch as your life unfolds with ever-increasing purpose and fulfillment. With heartfelt encouragement and unwavering faith, I believe in your ability to become the ideal human you have always aspired to be.

The Power Lies within You. Seize it, Own it, and Transform your LIFE.

The Stage is Set. The Curtains are Drawn. It's Time to BEGIN.

The World Awaits your Magnificent AWAKENING.

Tarrent-'Authur' Henry

Meet the Author

Tarrent-Arthur Henry writes under the name Tarrent-'Authur' Henry is a husband and step-father of two wonderful young men.

He is a member of Forbes BLK and he was named along with his wife, Helen, as one of Success Magazine's 125 most influential entrepreneurs of 2022.

Henry was also one of the featured Authors in De Mode Magazine in 2023.

He is the founder and guiding force of 'Righteous Uplifting Nourishing International, Inc. a 501c3 Non-Profit Organization whose global mission is to empower people by showing them how to make themselves and the world a better place.

He is a Best-Selling Author, Poet, Pastor, Chaplain, Mental Wellness Specialist, and a Certified Coach, Speaker, Teacher, Trainer, and Facilitator with Maxwell Leadership.

His best-selling book, "The Greatest Truth in the Universe" is making a difference in people's lives all around the world.

To Contact the Author:

Email Address:

info@authurhenry.com

Website:

www.authurhenry.com

www.intlrun.org.

Unlock Your True Potential - Become the Ideal Human in 90 Days! Are you mentally, emotionally, physically, and spiritually unwell and longing to be the best version of yourself? Do you feel like you must jump through hoops to have a strong relationship with God? Your life can change in just 90 days with my coaching program. You'll learn the tools to become mentally, emotionally, physically, and spiritually well with a strong relationship with God. You'll learn how to be the ideal human you've always wanted to be without having to jump through hoops. My program is designed to help you unlock your true potential and become the best version of yourself. Don't let another day go by feeling unwell and longing to be the ideal human. Start your transformation today and become the ideal human in just 90 days.

Go to my website www.authurhenry.com to get started and begin your journey towards becoming the ideal human.